8/30

J973.3

Long, John Cuthbert, 1892-
 The young revolutionaries [by] J.C. Long.
New York, J. Day [c1968]
 143p.   23cm.

 "A history of youthful heroes in the American Revolution."
 Bibliography: p. 141-143.

 1.U.S.-Hist.-Revolution-Juv. literature.
2.Revolutionists, American-Juv. literature.
 I.Title.
 J973.3 L

THE YOUNG REVOLUTIONARIES

This is the story of American youth who triggered the revolution against Great Britain.

Some were in their late teens when they started their agitation for freedom. Dozens of the leaders were in their twenties when they became publicly known as Rebels. George Washington was only twenty-seven when he first spoke out against British oppression.

The term "founding fathers" has erroneously created an impression of the revolutionaries as a group of graybeards.

Revolution obviously is led by persons. Hence, this story is told mainly as a collection of brief biographies of the gallant young men and women who challenged the authority of the Crown, a challenge in which they risked their lives if the cause should be lost.

It is the story, also, of the colleges as fomenters of revolt, for every campus was alive with agitation.

THE YOUNG
REVOLUTIONARIES

J. C. Long

The John Day Company

New York

Library of Congress Catalogue Card Number:
68-24151

PRINTED IN THE UNITED STATES OF AMERICA

To Alexander P. Clark
Curator of Manuscripts
Princeton University Library

Contents

THE YOUNG REVOLUTIONARIES

CHAPTER I

Andrew Jackson

The Youngest Famous Rebel

A T the age of thirteen, the youngest famous colonial took part in the Battle of Hanging Rock, on the southern border of North Carolina. His name was Andrew Jackson.

This was the same Andrew Jackson who many years later became President of the United States. Most of the early Presidents of the Republic had been fighters for the American cause in their twenties, or earlier. As far as is known, Andrew Jackson was the youngest Rebel in the Revolutionary forces; certainly he was the best-known one.

The story of young Andrew reveals the active part played by some of the Southern states in the American Revolution, notably North and South Carolina. The histories have had more to say about Massachusetts, Pennsylvania, and Virginia as leaders in the Revolution, and they were indeed leaders. Nevertheless, the two Carolinas were active in their desire for independence from the British Crown. Andrew became involved during his boyhood; he was forced into the war when his area was attacked by British forces under unexpected circumstances.

Andrew's father had emigrated from near Carrickfergus in Northern Ireland in the 1760's with his wife and two children. After visiting various areas, they settled in a little community named Waxhaw, which was partly in each of the Carolinas, and not far from the town of Charlotte, which was one of the largest places in that area. Andrew was born in Waxhaw on March 15, 1767. While he was still a young boy, his father died, leaving him and two brothers to be the defenders of the family.

Initially, there seemed to be little danger, as most of the fighting had been in the North. The Southern states had sent delegates to the Continental Congresses, and a group of citizens at Mecklenburg, North Carolina, had published a Declaration of Independence, but that had not been acted upon seriously by the other colonies. The major fighting of General Washington's forces had been in the North.

The Tory Cabinet in Great Britain had hoped that the bulk of the American colonists, especially the important ones, would oppose independence and remain loyally subject to the British Crown. This hope had been disappointed, but the Cabinet still believed that the South, except for Virginia, could be counted on to rally to the King's forces. The reason for so much misinformation in London was that most of the officialdom in the colonies was made up of appointments by the Cabinet or forces under royal control, and the appointees in America, probably sincerely, sent back reports which would be pleasing to the home offices.

There were many sympathizers in the British Parliament who admired the Americans for standing up for their rights as Englishmen, but the sympathizers in Parliament were out of power and did not control policy.

The war had been going badly for the Redcoats in various Northern battles, and Lord Cornwallis, the British commander, decided that he needed some Southern victories, especially to be able to send some good news to the home government.

He believed, evidently sincerely, that all he needed to do was to send troops into the South and the loyal Southerners would rise to his aid. Hence, he marched south with Tarleton and other officers, expecting a triumphal journey. Furthermore, he believed that his troops would be able to live off the country, that they would be welcomed and provided with supplies. To his dismay, he found that the countryside did not welcome his troops, that the colonials concealed their cattle and other supplies as far as possible.

Whereupon Cornwallis and his forces changed their objective to a march of conquest, with the aim of obliterating colonial forces. A detachment arrived in the Waxhaw area.

Andrew Jackson, with his brothers and cousins, rallied to the defense of the community, and thus it was that he became involved in the Battle of Hanging Rock, a site near at hand. This was a four-hour action, which has been described as one of the most hotly contested of the war. The Rebels had twelve killed and forty-one wounded, while the British admitted a loss of one hundred and ninety-two.

From then on, the Redcoats, particularly under the leadership of Tarleton, carried on a policy of annihilation. Their aim was to stamp out any Rebel resistance and carry on a war of frightfulness which would terrify the colonials into submission.

One defeated colonial group surrendered to Tarleton, asking for quarter. When they surrendered, Tarleton killed one hundred and thirteen outright, and wounded one hundred and fifty others. Hence, he won the nickname of Butcher Tarleton.

On one occasion, while Andrew Jackson was a prisoner, a British officer demanded that Andrew clean his boots. The boy protested that that could not be required of him as a prisoner of war, whereupon the officer slashed his hand to the bone; Jackson carried the scar through the rest of his life. It was following this incident that he was required to march forty miles to a British jail, where he was stripped of all his possessions.

13

Andrew's mother was a formidable woman. She somehow had contact with some colonial forces who had captured a number of British troops, and she managed to exchange her two sons and five neighbors for thirteen British soldiers.

Happily for Andrew, various American victories ensued not long after these events. Jackson luckily went through the rest of the war without serious troubles, and he remained its youngest hero.

The subsequent years for Andrew were a series of steady triumphs. He began to seek an education. He went first to the equivalent of a grade school, conducted by a Dr. Humphries. It is next reported that he attended Queens College in Charlotte. He went on to study law and for a time taught school before entering into law practice. The rest is history, but his early days are significant because, as did most of our Presidents, he valued schooling, and education had a large part in his success in life.

The choice of Andrew Jackson as an opening example in this book is due to the fact that he was an active fighter at an earlier age than others who were destined to be leaders in colonial protest and in the subsequent formation of a new country. Jackson was not, however, the youngest boy soldier. Virtually all the population, including boys and girls, were involved in the struggle. The British Army did not limit itself to formal battles, but spread out through the countryside following a scorched-earth policy. Every colonial family was in danger of being attacked, its cattle taken, and its lives endangered. Who actually was the youngest boy to carry a gun probably is not known. The Daughters of the American Revolution have listed Nathan Futrell as being the youngest drummer boy in the Revolution, having served in the North Carolina Continental Militia at the age of seven. He is buried in southwestern Kentucky, in an area taken for recreational development by the Tennessee Valley Authority.

There were many boys involved in the conflict. They were very

14

useful to the American cause in deceiving the enemy, acting as presumably loyal scouts but actually leading the Redcoats into false paths, giving them erroneous directions, and indulging in other deceptions.

There is a book on the subject entitled *Boys in the Revolution,* by Jack Coggins. The book gives three examples of young warriors in their early teens—John Greenwood, Ebenezer Fox, and Joseph Martin. All three behaved heroically and were doubtless useful to the cause, but no one of them became a leading factor in the Revolution.

CHAPTER II

Nathan Hale

Young Men Blaze the Way

So much has been written about the "founding fathers" of the United States that one gets the impression of wise old graybeards assembled in Congress debating the question of independence. Yet the leadership of the revolt against Britain had been stimulated long before 1776 by young people who blazed the way.

George Washington, "the father of his country," was only twenty-seven when he entered the Virginia House of Burgesses and took part in the resolutions of that body, denouncing the oppressions of the British Crown.

Patrick Henry was in his twenties when he rose in the same body and thundered, "Caesar had his Brutus, Charles the First his Cromwell, and George the Third—" The Speaker of the house interrupted to say that such a remark was treasonable. Henry retorted: "If this be treason, make the most of it!"

For more than a decade before the Declaration of Independence, various actions of Parliament and the Crown had been oppressive to the colonists, and it was the young men who spoke out most boldly. John Hancock was only twenty-nine when he was elected to the Massachusetts legislature on a campaign which sought to redress the wrongs imposed upon the colonists by the home government.

The Tory leaders, including His Majesty, had a totally different concept of the status of their American subjects from the view held by the colonials. In the eyes of the Tories the colonists existed for the benefit of the home government. They were, in effect, provinces populated by second-class citizens whose whole economy should be subject to the convenience and profit of the British enterprises. For example, the finest trees in Maine were selected by Crown agents to provide masts for the British fleet. The navigation laws were drawn to the disadvantage of colonial shipping. The Tories were quite sincere in their view; these oppressions were regarded as natural and proper by the home government, or rather by the Tory wing.

The attitude of the colonists was diametrically different. They considered themselves Englishmen, having equal status and equal rights with their relatives across the Atlantic. The patronizing attitude from the home country was intolerable. A peaceful adjustment of the differences might have been worked out. George Washington thought so, and for a long time proclaimed that he sought not independence but justice. The Whig leaders in Parliament took the same view, and openly sided with various American petitions for redress.

Unfortunately for any spirit of compromise, the Throne was badly misled by its own officers in the colonies. General Wolfe had denounced the Americans as a dirty, cowardly lot. The British general, Gage, had written the home office that the Bostonians were a mere rabble and that the presence of only two regiments would bring them to their knees.

The young revolutionaries at the outset apparently did not have outstanding influence. The high places in the Army, Navy, and custom houses were held by British appointees. An American colonial in the armed forces was outranked by a British officer holding the same grade of commission. The colonists resented the many discriminations against them, but the power of the Tories prevailed. although the young colonial leaders continued to agitate and would not be stilled.

One of the peculiar difficulties of the British Government was a lack of comprehension of the different characteristics of the diverse colonies, while making the attempt to legislate for all of them and continuously without their consent.

The Board of Trade, the Cabinet, the Tory majority in Parliament, and the Crown all took a hand from time to time in regulatory or punitive measures. The attempt to force the Bostonians into submission to unwelcome rulings was singularly ill-advised because the Massachusetts Bay Colony and the Plymouth Colony were founded by dissenters from the outset and to a large extent had regulations dictated by the authority of the Congregational Church. As most persons know, the Crown's attempt to teach Boston a lesson as an example to the other colonies proved a mistake.

The other major miscalculation on the part of the home government was to believe that in the Carolinas, especially South Carolina, the population could be relied upon to be completely Loyalist. On the surface there was calm. For example, the Church of England, together with the officers of the Crown, had the population under control. Every subject was obliged to pay a tax to the Established Church even though he worshiped elsewhere.

Furthermore, the leading colonists were wealthy men and were thus assumed to be conservative. The sons of many of them were sent to England to be educated and were expected to become devoted loyal Englishmen.

However, Charleston was not exclusively English either in its population or in its sympathies. It was the most cosmopolitan city in the New World. It was inhabited by French Huguenots, Germans and other Lutherans, Czech bankers, a few Spanish, and some Dutch.

The Huguenots were the most powerful single group. Originally they had been driven out of France because they were Protestant. Many had fled to England, where they met with hospitality and contributed to the upbuilding of various handicrafts. When a considerable number of them emigrated to South Carolina they were predisposed in favor of England, but the home government with typical stupidity enforced legislation that was singularly irritating to the Huguenots. The point at issue was the decision mentioned above that every inhabitant must pay a tax for the support of the Church of England.

Religion was a particularly tender subject with the Huguenots. Their theological views were similar to those of the Established Church, but they decided to organize their own congregation with their own form of worship and their own clergy drawn from the Huguenot colony. They held services in French and English, and they put up their own building on the same streets as the first English church. The edifice was a gem of Gothic beauty, worthy of the group who had made it possible. The Huguenots were prosperous and educated, leaders in the community. They included such families as Ravenal and St. Julien.

Since the Huguenots had formed and organized a coherent congregation, they felt themselves to be entitled to equal status with the English church, from a civic standpoint and felt that they should be exempt from the tax imposed by that church. Their request for such relief was flatly refused; hence they were under the necessity of bearing the expense of their own congregation plus the tax of the English church. This was a constant source of discontent.

Charleston and its surrounding countryside was teeming with prosperity in the decades shortly before the Revolution. Many of its people were independently wealthy, and they were not of the character to be pushed around. Numerous families had large estates raising cattle, sheep, and produce, and displayed elaborate landscaping such as that of the Middleton Gardens. Rice, indigo, and long-staple cotton were among the rich crops.

Two of the sons of these families who were to become conspicuous in the Rebel cause were Edward Rutledge and Arthur Middleton. Each was sent abroad when of preparatory school age to attend English academies. From then on, each studied law at the Middle Temple in London. They became deeply saturated with the concepts of English law, which revealed to them that the regulations imposed upon South Carolina were extralegal and unjust. They returned to Charleston and immediately became advocates of colonial self-rule. They were among the younger protesters against the Stamp Act, which was passed in 1765. Rutledge and Middleton were in their twenties then. Their influence was potent, for they were among the most eligible young men in Charleston. Later, they were among the young signers of the Declaration of Independence.

North Carolina originally was under the same judicial rule as the southern area. It was not as prosperous as South Carolina and did not have identical grievances, but its population was intrinsically alien to the English. It had been founded largely by Scottish immigrants, who had fled from Great Britain. Many had come over at the time of the failure of the Stuart uprising. Flora Macdonald, at the age of twenty-two, had helped the Stuart leader, Prince Charles Edward, to escape the British pursuit after the collapse of the Stuart revolt at Culloden. She herself fled to America, and was a local heroine. The population was grimly resentful of rule from

20

across the water. In its growing resentment, leaders began to arise. William Hooper was one of the most outspoken representatives of the colony, protesting against the Stamp Act when he was only twenty-three. He also became a signer of the Declaration.

It is natural for the younger element in every population from their late teens onward to be against the establishment, whatever form it may take. But in the domestic life of the colonies the establishment itself, namely the wealthy classes, was against British rule and on the side of young protest. Hence the attention of those who wanted change was directed toward striking off the shackles imposed by Great Britain. Reform and change were not the exclusive domain of the young. Benjamin Franklin, obviously an outstanding genius of his time, was sixty years of age at the time of the Stamp Act Congress, a body of men from several of the provinces who made a start toward unity that resulted finally in the Continental Congresses which led to the Declaration. Samuel Adams was a veteran in the cause. James Otis, born in 1725, was one of the oldest Revolutionary statesmen.

One of the youngest and most popular patriots was Nathan Hale, descendant of a man who had come to America in 1632 and founded a family of great distinction. Nathan's father was a farmer, and like many New England farmers he put a high value on education. When his son showed an aptitude for learning and desired to go to college, his father encouraged him. The family lived in the small village of Coventry, Connecticut. The available schooling was limited, but Nathan was taken under the tutelage of the local minister, an excellent classical scholar. In those days the preacher frequently was the most learned man in his community. He was sure to be versed in Latin, Greek, Hebrew, and English grammar. He would be acquainted with the Bible and the works of Shakespeare. He was quite likely to be a man of urbanity and wit, and

21

this was the case with Nathan's tutor. Though there were doubtless dour men in the pulpit, of the Jonathan Edwards stripe, this was not typical.

At any rate, Nathan entered Yale at the age of fourteen and became a student of prodigious accomplishment and the founder of a literary society. Moreover, young Hale excelled in virtually every activity. He seems like a figure of fiction, so large were his interests and accomplishments. He took a broad jump on the Yale Common which so astounded the people that the distance was marked and shown to visitors as a local curiosity. He could kick a football farther and higher than any of his colleagues. One of his favorite recreations was to go down the road and kick his football over the tops of the highest trees. He was also a popular wrestler, ready to take on all comers. Even before his graduation from college he had become a legend up and down the Atlantic Coast.

Though there were no railroads, telegraph, telephones, or other means of rapid communication, the colonies kept well informed of each other through the medium of the postboys and intercolonial trade. A stagecoach and/or men on horseback carried the news. There were taverns at the end of a day's journey all the way from Maine to South Carolina. Hence the word was passed along from province to province regarding any items of interest. The exploits of Nathan Hale were a familiar subject in the colonies. Quite possibly they lost nothing in the retelling, and at any rate, he became the young hero throughout the whole seaboard.

He also was a well-built, handsome youth with a fair skin, blue eyes, and flaxen hair. He had an outgiving personality and liked people, including the girls. And with it all he was an idealist.

Upon finishing his studies at Yale he taught school in East Haddam, Connecticut, and the following year he taught in New London until July, 1775.

He was a Patriot from the beginning, and when he received news of the Battle of Lexington he rose in the New London town meeting and made an impassioned speech on behalf of liberty and independence. Shortly after this event he volunteered for the Colonial Army and was created a lieutenant by the General Assembly of Connecticut. After a brief training he joined the Continental Army under Washington at Cambridge, Massachusetts, and participated in the siege of Boston. When Washington's army withdrew to New York and was in a sorry state of disorganization, the general called for a volunteer to go behind the lines of the British encamped on Long Island and find out what their plans might be. The task of being a spy was not appealing—it usually meant death if one were caught—but Hale volunteered. When a friend tried to dissuade him he said, "I wish to be useful and every kind of service necessary to the public good becomes honorable by being necessary."

Nathan Hale went to the British encampment, got his information, and was returning to New York to Washington's headquarters on Harlem Heights. He had almost reached the encampment when he was caught by British soldiers and taken to British Commander Howe.

It is probable that he was betrayed by a fellow American with Tory sympathies, for his apprehending appeared to be no accident. Maps and other papers were on his person when he was captured. He made no further concealment, but gave his name, his rank as a captain in the American Army and his object in coming within the British lines.

Possibly he hoped that giving his rank as a commissioned officer might lead to his being treated as a prisoner of war. The British commander, however, decreed, without the form of a trial, that Hale should be hanged the following day. There was no thought of exchanging him as a prisoner of war or of sparing his life. The execution took place as planned. As the rope was thrown around his neck Nathan Hale made a spirited address which is said to have concluded with the words: "I only regret that I have but one life to lose for my country."

The news spread through the colonies like wildfire. "Did you know that they hanged Nathan Hale?" the stagecoach passengers would say on arriving at a tavern. The departing coaches would carry the news to their destinations.

"They hanged Nathan Hale. They hanged Nathan Hale," was the refrain throughout the countryside. Men and women wept openly. "They hanged Nathan Hale? Oh, it can't be!" But, of course, it was the fact, grim and bitter, intended to disgrace not only Hale but the dignity of every colonial. The event made an impression, though not the one intended by the Tory government. From that point on the determination of the revolutionists was to carry on to the very end until the sacrifice of Nathan Hale was redeemed.

CHAPTER III

Alexander Hamilton

Nineteen-Year-Old Orator

W HEN young Hamilton first came to America and attended grammar school in Elizabethtown, New Jersey, William Livingston and Elias Boudinot made themselves his foster parents. He entered King's College in New York (now Columbia University) at the age of sixteen. He studied hard, participated actively in a small discussion seminar with other students in which many of the issues of the day were aired, and is said to have been extremely popular with the students.

There seems to be some question as to just how Hamilton was converted to the Patriot cause. The *Dictionary of American Biography* says that from the time he was a guest of William Livingston, he accepted the Patriot views. On the other hand, *Lamb's Dictionary of American Biography* says that his conversion to the Patriot cause came after a visit to Boston in 1774, at which time he interviewed the leaders of the Revolutionary movement. Other biographers suggest that his strong feelings for the Patriots may have come about through his discussions with fellow collegians.

The imagination of most youths is kindled at the name of Liberty, and perhaps that was reason enough for Hamilton to become interested and involved, along with many other college students. What made him stand out was the skill, the force, and the judgment with which he defended his position.

There is one event upon which all the sources seem to agree, and this event apparently launched him into full involvement in the Patriot cause. This occasion was a mass meeting in The Fields in New York City (now City Hall Park). When the speaker (in Hamilton's opinion) failed to deal with the real issues, Hamilton mounted the platform uninvited and made an eloquent speech in behalf of colonial rights that reached the hearts of his listeners and forced the Tory Assembly to declare its position on the great question of the day. Soon afterward, he anonymously wrote two pamphlets, "A Full Vindication" and "The Farmer Refuted," and so convincing were his arguments that the authorship was credited to John Jay and other well-known patriot writers. Hamilton's position at this time was that of a moderate, who loyally defended the King's sovereignty and the British connection, but rejected the pretensions of Parliament. His speech in The Fields and the writing of these two pamphlets were accomplished in his seventeenth year, to the amazement of many intellectuals of the day, including Dr. Myles Cooper, president of King's College.

Early in 1776, when he was barely nineteen, he was given command of an artillery company by the New York Convention, and did such an excellent job with it that General Greene's attention was drawn to him. General Greene recommended him to General Washington as someone with outstanding qualities, perhaps someone Washington might want for his staff. Some time later, he did become General Washington's aide.

How he came to do so, in fact how he came to be in New York at all, seems like a miracle.

Nevis in the Leeward Islands of the West Indies was the birth-place of Alexander Hamilton in 1757. The circumstances of his young boyhood were a handicap. His enemies always alleged that he was a bastard, and it is true that the marriage of his parents was never made legal even though they were accepted in the society of Nevis as a respectable married couple.

The confusion began with the self-willed conduct of Alexander's mother. She was a daughter of a leading citizen of Nevis who was a doctor and a prominent planter.

Two other Leeward Islands, St. Croix and St. Kitts, were closely related to Nevis both by family connections and trade. When Alexander's mother, Rachel, was only sixteen, she was taken to visit relatives in St. Croix. While there she met a young Dane who had just settled on the island and was looking for a wife. Rachel's mother thought that this was a fine chance to get a daughter married off as early as sixteen. Rachel did not think so, but the mother insisted. The marriage was unhappy from the start and was not made any easier by the birth of a son, during which time Rachel was critically ill. She turned the baby over to her husband and fled to her father's house in Nevis seeking a divorce. A divorce was obtainable only by a special ruling of the Council, and they were unwilling to pass the special act which would have been contrary to British practice (Nevis was a British colony).

While this matter was under discussion a young James Hamilton visited Nevis. He had a store at nearby St. Kitts and he, too, was looking for a wife. (Rachel had lived intermittently at St. Kitts).

James was a younger son of a British family and had emigrated to the New World hoping to find opportunity there. Rachel found him charming and consented to marry him, disregarding the fact that her divorce had not yet come through as she had hoped. The young couple lived together happily for some time in a pleasant house where Alexander was born. Apparently their bills were paid by Rachel's father.

James Hamilton had no business sense. Rachel advanced him large sums of money which he lost in various enterprises. His store went broke and he became penniless, unable to support his family.

For Rachel this circumstance was a sad disillusion. Taking Alexander with her, she went again to St. Croix where she lived with wealthy relatives. James departed to a neighboring island, where he subsisted mostly on neighborly charity for the rest of his life.

At the age of eleven, it was necessary for Alexander to work, and he took a job in a local general store, but he could see little future in St. Croix. The island had only one major industry, the growth and processing of sugar cane. Unless one had the money to own substantial acres, there was no future in sugar. The boy, however, was filled with ambition. He was conscious of having an unusual mind. He learned to speak French fluently and contributed writings to the local newspaper.

One of these reports stimulated the interest in him of a well-to-do aunt. She put up the money to send him to America when he was only fifteen. He entered the grammar school at Elizabethtown, New Jersey and was ready for college at the age of sixteen. While he was in college, he made the acquaintance of trustees and other influential persons on the campus.

The New York upper-class citizens were not by temperament rebellious. They represented money and privilege and liked it that way. The Dutch had been the first settlers. Many of their leading families had castles on the Hudson. It seems quite amazing that this ambitious young man was able to move into the society of these wealthy burghers, but he did. One of his major moves from a worldly standpoint (and we do not deny that it also may have been romantic) was to marry a daughter of General Philip Schuyler, who had distinguished himself in the French and Indian Wars, and who was also one of the wealthiest men in the colony. From the time of his engagement to Miss Schuyler, the vigorous young man, in a modern phrase, "had it made."

But he had no intention of allowing the Schuylers and the Livingstons to run him. Quite the reverse. Indeed, all through the years of the Declaration, the formative states of the Republic, and the final drawing up of the Constitution, we find New York's leaders grumbling, muttering, and dubious but prevailed upon by Alexander Hamilton.

He personally was brave. He desired to fight, and he volunteered when war began. As mentioned above, he applied for command of an artillery company when he was still only nineteen, and received it. While he had at one time defended the sovereignty of the English King, though rejecting the authority of Parliament, he now joined forces unreservedly with George Washington and fought throughout the Battle of Long Island, commanded guns at White Plains, and was in the retreat through New Jersey. He longed for military glory and fortunately was observed by George Washington, who made him his secretary and aide-de-camp, with the rank of lieutenant colonel. In this post he was of great value to Washington, because Hamilton had a genius for administration and paper work. When victory finally had been won, it was clear that Hamilton would be one of the first men of the Republic.

It should be said that there was strong sentiment for liberty among the masses in the city of New York. This was in contrast to the stolidity of the upper classes. The Society of Tammany was originally an organization for protest. The Sons of Liberty likewise clamored for independence, not from Britain alone but from any imposition of authority. Some of the more conservative elements characterized demonstrations by these bodies as "mob rule" and tried to identify the Revolutionary cause with a spirit of unrest.

Leaders of the forthcoming Revolution, however, were not drawn from the mob. In virtually every instance they were sons of the elite. In short, those families who had been the leading influences in the colonial days continued to supply the young leaders for the new cause. A great mistake of the Tories was to assume that the persons of "the establishment" in America would intrinsically be on their side.

CHAPTER IV

Young John Hancock

The Wealthiest Rebel in His Early Years

JOHN HANCOCK, who was graduated from Harvard at the age of seventeen, in 1754, was perhaps the most famous of the young Revolutionaries.

He was not so young when he signed the Declaration of Independence. He was thirty-nine then, yet still not a graybeard. As any American school boy or girl probably knows, it was the Hancock signature which led all the rest in a big flourishing hand at the head of the signers of the Declaration; and he said, "I guess George the Third can read that without his specs!"

It may be less well remembered that there was a price on Hancock's head at the time. He had been involved in every famous Rebel move for twenty years. He had been the instigator of the Boston Tea Party. He had helped to plan Paul Revere's ride. He had been an organizer of the Massachusetts Provincial Congress, a prelude to the original Continental Congress. In the eyes of the British, Hancock was the number one bad boy.

Hancock had started life with a superiority complex which had given him self-confidence. His father was the Congregational minister at Braintree, Massachusetts. Many ministers' sons feel a certain security above that of, say, the banker's son or the son of the leading merchant, for the minister is the vicar of the Almighty. In theatrical parlance, "You can't top that."

However, John's father died when the boy was still young, and he was adopted by a childless uncle. The uncle was probably the richest man in the province. He owned a fleet of sailing ships and did a large export and import business. He also owned various real estate properties in the Boston area. His name was Thomas Hancock, and he was revered as one of the ablest men in the colony. He had complete confidence in his young nephew, soon made him a partner, and also made him the principal beneficiary of his will.

While Hancock was still in his twenties, his uncle died, leaving John the business, his sailing ships, and a quantity of cash totaling £700,000, possibly the equivalent of $3,000,000.

Early in his career, young Hancock made a visit to England. While there he was treated with outstanding courtesy. He was recognized as the most important financial man in Massachusetts, and he possibly could have become a money power in Great Britain and been elevated to the peerage. It was customary for a man who gave large sums to the party in power to be honored with a place in the House of Lords.

Hancock, however, was a true colonial. He had no desire to affiliate with the British establishment, and from his early days he used his influence in trying to get recognition for the rights of the colonies, most especially in Massachusetts. This colony was bearing the brunt of persecution from the Crown. There was a distribution of powerful elements in the province. The Massachusetts Bay Colony was largely the instrument of the Congregational Church. The Pilgrims dominated the Plymouth area. The British Government was the actual ruler of the province, and Governor Gage was the active head. Gage initially looked upon Hancock with favor, and created him a colonel on his staff. That lasted until Hancock was known to be active against the policies of the home government, at which time his commission was removed.

The difference with the home government came to a head with the passage of the Stamp Act. This Act imposed a tax on various products bought by the colonies, who had had no voice in the imposition of the tax. Hancock had spoken out boldly against the measure. A ship loaded with tea came into Boston Harbor. A group of men disguised as Indians boarded the ship, seized the containers of tea, and dumped them overboard into the harbor. This event came to be known as the Boston Tea Party, and it was alleged that Hancock was one of the men disguised as Indians.

He was constantly active on many fronts, but not the least of his problems was trying to avoid the eager young ladies of the area. As the richest bachelor anywhere around, he was naturally the target of ambitious mamas. One of those whom he could not avoid was his Aunt Lydia, who was promoting the cause of Dorothy Quincy. For some months he avoided an engagement, but he finally succumbed. Shortly afterward, he quarreled with the young woman and the match was broken off. However, Aaron Burr arrived on the scene and paid court to Dorothy. That reactivated Hancock's interest, so that he renewed his courtship ardently and married the girl.

The marriage was a great success, thought touched with tragedy. Both a girl and a boy were born to the couple, but each died young. Hancock's devotion to his wife is illustrated by a letter which he wrote to her, which as far as is known has never previously been published. It came to her from Rhode Island, probably when Hancock was leading an unsuccessful military expedition against the British in that area. It is addressed: "To Mrs. Hancock, near the Common, Boston," and it says:

My Dear Dotty

We have an exceeding heavy storm, but I am most conveniently situated, have a charming house, with rooms to myself & my gentlemen, & the family of the house devoted to us. I hope this will find you well. I shall soon see you. Remember me to Doc Cooper* & all friends. I wish you could step in & see us, I assure you we live in taste, I keep a publick table, & am determined to support the honours of the state as far as I can. Remember me to my Brother & Sister, to Mrs. Brackett, & pray kiss our little Son for me.

God bless you, my sweet girl. I am with the most solid affection & real love,

Yours for ever
John Hancock

We have gotten ahead of our story because Hancock actually was thirty-nine before he found time to get married. That was obviously late in any era, and particularly in colonial times it was late for a first marriage.

Hancock, in spite of his wealth, was extremely popular, for he was a humanitarian and very free-handed with his money. Any family in financial distress could expect some help from him. He respected the rights of Negroes, and advocated that they should have full privileges of citizenship, which was quite rare for a man of his time. In fact, toward the freedmen there was no discrimination in schools, restaurants, or public services.

As long as the British Government ruled Massachusetts, Hancock was free from official persecution. A group of Redcoats tried to burn down his house but were driven off. Gage, the British governor, apologized and said that this was no doing on his part.

---

* Rev. Samuel Cooper, D.D., an active patriot, pastor of a leading Boston church.

He was wise to take that stand, as the Boston mob was unruly and could readily have burned the governor's mansion.

Hancock's popularity was increased by another outrage visited upon him by the British administration. One of his ships, *Liberty*, was charged with smuggling in a large cargo of Madeira wine. Smuggling was a frequent activity of the colonials, who resented import taxes which had been imposed without their consent. There seems to have been no doubt about the guilt of the *Liberty,* and when she set sail on her next voyage she was seized by the British authorities. She was condemned, transferred to the British Coast Guard, and towed to Newport, Rhode Island, where she was attacked and burned by a colonial mob. The entire incident cast Hancock in the popular role of martyr.

The British sympathizers sneered at Hancock for his dandified ways. He customarily wore the most elaborate and expensive clothes. He entertained lavishly. He frequently would have twenty persons or more to dinner, and he made little distinction as to social class. Upper-crust families, British toadies, and others looked askance at him and his ways, but the general public thought he was wonderful. He was a Robin Hood of the day: he did not rob the rich, because he was rich himself, but he gave to the poor lavishly.

He obviously was considered a bulwark of the colonial cause because Paul Revere stayed at the Hancock home the night before he began his famous.ride. In fact, that was only one of the many offenses that could be charged against Hancock, if the British had ever been able to lay their hands on him, or if the Revolution had failed.

General Washington took command of the Revolutionary Army at Cambridge, Massachusetts. This galled Hancock because he had been a candidate for that job and considered himself the most prominent man in the Revolution. In point of fact, he had no military experience except for some unsuccessful sorties in Rhode Island. However, he supported Washington, and when the British were being driven out of Boston, Hancock lent his support to the burning of Boston, even though he owned many properties there and the result was costly for him.

With the removal of the British, Massachusetts had self-government, headed by a general court. Hancock was elected to it, and when it formed a provincial congress he was chosen president, and chairman of the committee of safety, with power to call out the militia. He was one of several especially *excluded* from an offer of amnesty made by the British.

When independence had been won, Hancock found himself in the position of the high schooler who moves on to a job or to college, or to the college man once graduation has propelled him into new fields. In short, Hancock was now safe. No longer a price on his head, he was in a new world. His glamorous youth was gone and—great irony—he had the gout. That made his enemies laugh and embarrassed his political friends.

However, Hancock's popularity in his home state remained untarnished. In Massachusetts, his youthful bravery and his continuing generosity to the public were appreciated. Hancock was elected nine times as governor of his state, a political record rarely approached anywhere. He never lost favor with the populace, though he occasionally offended the nabobs. He was chosen treasurer of Harvard College, and refused to give accountability to its overseers. That was indefensible, of course, and he and his estate finally settled all accounts.

Hancock's last great contribution to the nation was to bring the pivotal state of Massachusetts to support the new national Constitution.

CHAPTER V

Young Women of the Revolution

Molly Pitcher and Betsy Ross

Abigail Smith and Dorothy Quincy were each seventeen years old when they set their caps for leaders of the colonial rebellion.

The term is perhaps unfair, because in each case the girl was egged on by other members of her family. The circumstances also were different because Abigail had an ardent suiter in the person of John Adams, whereas Dorothy's intended, John Hancock, had no desire to get married at all. In fact he strongly rebuked his aunt, who was trying to promote the match.

In each case the seventeen-year-old got her man and ultimately became one of the famous women of the Revolution. The story of each is illuminating as it shows how engagements may be tumultuous and yet end in a happy marriage.

Abigail's father, Rev. William Smith, was minister of the church at Weymouth, Massachusetts. In the Congregational hierarchy of the time the pastor of the village church was the leading citizen of the community. Mrs. Smith looked for an eminent match for her daughter, possibly some other clergyman not yet married. At any rate she had little regard for John Adams, at that time an impecunious lawyer.

The father was more realistic and approved of the young attorney. However, the courtship lasted three years before the marriage took place. Abigail had a keen mind and brought out the best in her husband. When he ultimately became the United States ambassador to Great Britain, the Adamses made a distinguished couple.

Dorothy Quincy came originally from Braintree, Massachusetts. Her chief sponsor was an aunt of John Hancock, who acted at times as the chatelaine of his household and apparently was the only woman who dared to scold him. Dorothy was a girl of outstanding beauty. She had reddish-gold hair, green eyes, and a handsome figure. Aunt Lydia told Hancock that the girl was a prize and that he would do well to grab her quickly before someone else did. Hancock protested that mothers with eligible daughters were always trying to ensnare him and that all they wanted was his money. He said he had no time for a woman in his life. Between his active business and his duties with the general court of the province his days were crowded to the hilt. He asked her to leave him alone. She told him that he was a crusty, selfish person and would get worse as time went on if he did not have some woman to normalize his life.

It is not clear how actively Dorothy did or did not take part in this campaign. The fact that Aunt Lydia had the free run of his house and could invite her protégée there at any time evidently helped the cause. At any rate, Hancock succumbed, and as told earlier, the marriage was a happy one and he became an ardently devoted husband.

The women of the Revolution were, for the most part, unsung heroines. Very few were famous. They were not supposed to enlist in the Army or become members of the provincial congress.

Nevertheless theirs was a heavy burden. They needed to keep the farms going while the men were away at war, and the chief occupation of the colonials was farming. Also, their sympathies in general must have been with the colonial cause. Women are supposedly conservative, and it might be thought that the colonial women would be entranced by the glamour of the King and court. However, the colonial wives were pioneers, not sheltered daughters, and were face to face with the realities of existence.

The colonial women realized the importance of independence and resented the presence of Redcoats swarming over the countryside. Often they were called upon to be the defenders of their homes when the husbands were away at war. British General Tarleton believed in carrying on a war of frightfulness, a campaign of extinction. He would destroy everyone in any household that lay within his path, including the women and children. A woman's rifle was her only sure defense. Customarily, warfare in the eighteenth century was a game with certain understood rules and procedures, even to the extent of certain holidays being observed on both sides. That chivalrous attitude was not adopted toward the colonies; they were rebellious subjects who should be punished, hence they were involved not in a civilized war but in a battle for survival.

There were two women who achieved fame through their own direct efforts. One was the so-called Molly Pitcher, whose legal name was Mary Ludwig Hays. She was the daughter of John George Ludwig, who ran a dairy farm near Trenton, New Jersey. She became a servant in the family of Dr. William Irvine, of Carlisle, Pennsylvania. While there she married John Caspar Hays in 1769.

Hays enlisted in the First Pennsylvania Regiment and fought in the Battle of Monmouth, New Jersey, on June 28, 1778. Molly had accompanied her husband to the area, and since the day

39

was terrifically hot, she kept bringing pitchers of water to her husband and to the other soldiers. Most of the men did not know who she was and she became designated simply as Molly Pitcher.

Her husband fell to the ground, overcome by the heat, and she took his place by his cannon. She charged it and fired it repeatedly during the remainder of the battle. The story of her heroism is not merely legend, for after the war the General Assembly of Pennsylvania took note of her record and voted her a pension of forty dollars annually. Such was the history of Mrs. John Caspar Hayes, better known as Molly Pitcher.

Another notable woman of the Revolutionary period was Betsy Ross, who supposedly made the first American flag. She was born in Philadelphia in 1752, the daughter of Samuel and Rebecca Griscom. She attended the Friends' School on South Fourth Street and became a member of Quaker society. However, in 1773 she eloped to Gloucester, New Jersey, with John Ross, son of a Protestant minister. The Friends expelled her for "marrying out of meeting." Fortunately for her, there was a schism in that denomination and she subsequently became a member of the Society of Free Quakers.

Betsy was skillful at needlework and established a reputation in making flags for ships. The Pennsylvania State Navy Board recorded payments to her for making naval flags in 1777. The Stars and Stripes was adopted in June, 1777.

Legend has it that Betsy Ross made the Stars and Stripes at the request of George Washington and Robert Morris, the Philadelphia banker who did much to finance the Revolution.

The basis for this story is an address made by Betsy's grandson, William Canby, in a paper read before the Historical Society of Pennsylvania in March, 1870. There has been a disposition in some quarters to doubt this story on the basis that it comes to us only as a family tradition without any other supporting evidence. Yet there

40

seems to be no reason to disbelieve it. Presumably the Historical Society of Pennsylvania considered Canby to be a reliable citizen, and there is no reason to doubt his word. Betsy Ross was known to be a designer of flags, and she will go down in history as the designer of the Stars and Stripes.

There were doubtless many other women who had conspicuous parts in the Revolution, but since histories are written mostly by men and about men, not many women have become known to us through the printed page.

CHAPTER VI

The Strange Betrayal

Major André, Benedict Arnold, and Peggy Shippen

This chapter is written at considerable length because it is about the most controversial of the issues involving the American sympathies: Were they Royalist or Patriot? Was Benedict Arnold a voluntary traitor? Did Peggy Shippen cause him to be such? Was André an instigator of that betrayal? As we read the story it shows that the American public were pro-Patriot. Note that when André was apprehended his captors were simple American patriots. Throughout his imprisonment and court-martial there was no uprising of Loyalists among the people to clamor for his freedom.

THERE is a general impression that youth is idealistic; that young people are the ones who embrace new ideas, often in conflict with their stolid elders.

As a general proposition that is often true, but it is equally true that there is a conservative element among the young, who can be belligerently on the side of things that are. Specifically, it was a nineteen-year-old Philadelphian, Margaret Shippen, who became involved in the ill-fated ruin of Benedict Arnold; and Major John André was in his twenties when he first became acquainted with Peggy Shippen and with Arnold, who was the military commandant at Philadelphia.

The events which piled up one after the other had seemingly the inexorable movement of a Greek tragedy, as if directed from some outside sinister force, though the affair of Arnold and Peggy Shippen started in seeming innocence.

The situation in Philadelphia was uncertain. The government of the city had changed hands several times in several years. The British Army had occupied it, then British General Howe had withdrawn. Then the colonials were in the ascendancy and George Washington had appointed Arnold as commandant. This was essentially a temporary consolation prize, for Arnold had been a heroic fighting general on the colonial side and had been severely wounded in battle. His right leg had been almost shot away, leaving him unfit for action in the field, though it was expected that after some months of convalescence he would return to action.

The sympathies of the Philadelphians were divided. Those loyal to the Crown were in the majority, though sometimes there would be division of opinion in the same family. For example, most of Peggy Shippen's family were loyal to the Crown, but she had a brother who was a physician with the Continental Army. All of the population were British subjects, for the American Revolution was a civil war and so regarded at the time. The colonies felt that they had been driven to independence by the unjust acts of the home government, and up until the very end it was believed both in England and in America that the home government could and would make concessions that would reunite both sides.

The Shippen family had been prominent in the colony for more than a hundred years. They had originally been appointees of

William Penn and his successors, who had been proprietors of the colony. The Penns were the ruling authority of Pennsylvania, which they operated virtually as an independent state.

When Arnold was put in charge of Philadelphia he was close to forty. It was natural that he soon met Peggy Shippen. Arnold and Peggy were immediately attracted to each other. The situation was not unusual. A man approaching middle age is flattered if a charming young creature finds him attractive. A popular young girl, on the other hand, also is flattered if a distinguished older man finds her attractive. Such a man can be far more stimulating than the average run of youths of her own age. Benedict and Peggy became engaged in 1779 and soon were married.

The theory that Peggy was an agent of the Crown who had seduced Arnold into betraying his country was widely held, but was untrue. She followed the lead of her husband and probably sympathized with his ultimate disenchantment with the American cause, but she was not the prime instigator. Arnold, after his ulimate disgrace, never implicated Peggy. He stoutly maintained that she was an innocent party. It is known that a certain Major André was the chief plotter, who came into a situation in which all three parties were ripe for temptation. Arnold, Peggy, and André all had known considerable wealth, and in each case, through the failure of parents, prosperity had been swept away from them. As the apostle Paul said, "The love of money is the root of all evil." And the circumstances of each of the three made them eager to come into the possession of wealth.

The character of André was almost fictional. He was the embodiment of the character of the devil in Goethe's *Faust*—charming, persuasive, handsome, and a liar from the beginning. André's father was a Swiss merchant who had established a business in London. While in that city he met and married a French woman who was living in a community of French emigrés. Their son, John

44

André, was ultimately taken into his father's business, and at the age of nineteen he had a job in the accounting department which he found very boring. However, the business was highly prosperous, and it seemed probable that young André would be chained to a job in commerce for the rest of his life.

The young man's real interest, however, was in the arts. He could write poetry, paint, design women's hats, act on the stage, and create and direct pageants. Apparently he made no effort to pursue the arts professionally, perhaps because he had no time to do so while connected with his father's business. Suddenly, however, the old man died. The business rapidly declined, and André was free to leave home. Though born in England he had no British relatives, no connections to give him a lift up. The one career that seemed to be available was the Army, because it was possible to buy a commission. Hence, young André bought himself a second lieutenancy and soon was shipped over to America in an army of His Majesty.

While in America, before the Revolution broke out, he visited in Philadelphia and was an immediate social success. He put on plays, drew portraits of the ladies, and became a friend of the budding Peggy Shippen, who at sixteen had already become a social favorite.

After war broke out André became attached to the staff of Sir Henry Clinton, who succeeded Howe as commander of the British forces. Clinton made his headquarters in New York.

André promptly showed his skill as an army politician. He flattered Clinton, did odd jobs for him, relieved him of detail, and soon wormed his way into the position of indispensable man: anyone who desired to see Clinton had to make his appointments through André; persons desiring to sell supplies to Clinton had to see André. Ultimately André persuaded Clinton to appoint him as adjutant general with the rank of major. That appointment as

45

major seemed to be a protection for the future. If Clinton should be transferred or removed from office André's favorable situation at headquarters would vanish, but the post of a major in the regular Army would provide a lifetime income.

The appointment as major, however, soon ran into a snag. André had glibly told Clinton that he already had the rank of captain in the regular Army. That was a half-truth—General Howe, when commander in Philadelphia, had made the young man a captain on his staff, but it was not to be a permanent rank. Hence, the next step would be the rank of major. However, generals in the field were not authorized to make regular Army appointments. Lord George Germain, secretary for the Colonies, was surprised at this irregular move and asked George III what should be done about it. The King told Germain to get the opinion of General Jeffery Amherst, who at this time was head of the Army on the home front. Amherst, on being consulted, said that he had looked at his files, had gone through the list of captains, and did not find the name of André there. In fact, the name was completely unfamiliar, and he saw no grounds whatever in authorizing such a commission.

Outwardly, André received this report calmly, saying that there must be some mistake somewhere and that his rank as major might be continued on the American scene as long as he was in the service of Clinton.

Inwardly, André was frightened. His hopes for future security had been dashed. When the war was over and he was transferred elsewhere, he faced an unhappy decline in his fortunes. His rank would revert to lieutenancy, and his opportunities for fine graft in the general's office would be no more. He needed to create some master stroke which would commend him to the home government and possibly give him a rank above what he had dreamed of hitherto.

46

A daring idea crossed his mind. What if he could capture West Point? That was the chief fortress of the Continental Army. It guarded the entryway to the upper Hudson River. If that fort should fall into the hands of the British, the colonial cause would be virtually doomed. It was too strong a fortress to be taken by assault, and a long siege was impractical. The only way to get possession would be by betrayal. And the next question was how to get someone high enough in authority to be put in charge of the fort, and at the same time sufficiently open to temptation to be willing to sell out.

The present commander of the fort was a staunch colonial, and André had no personal contact with him, but as he cast about in his mind he wondered if he might work something out with Benedict Arnold.

Only a man with as devious a character as that of André could have dreamed up such a scheme. André was helped by the fact that he had no loyalties to any cause. He was not a colonial, of course, and his only ties with England were the fact that he had purchased his Army commission. His racial heritage was Swiss and French. That left him free to navigate in treacherous waters without any deterrent of conscience. The more he thought of his fantastic scheme, the more he favored Arnold as a possible prospect. One tradition is that Arnold made the initial approach, but that seems unlikely, as he had excellent financial picking within his Philadelphia command.

Arnold had become notoriously greedy for money in his Philadelphia post. As a young boy, he had lived in an elaborate home in Norwich, Connecticut. His mother had inherited a substantial fortune for those days. His father had run a prosperous apothecary shop. The shop was something like a modern drugstore, selling a multitude of products—not only drugs, but fans, notions of all sorts, patent medicines, perfumes, candies, and imported novelties from all over the world. Young Arnold was quite the top boy of the town when he was in his early teens. He also won prestige because he was the best athlete, a wrestler and diver, and a boy to be afraid of in a fight. He was no coward, as a matter of fact. He liked to pick on older boys because it was a challenge, and he would defend boys younger than himself, which made him a hero. His mother, as the wealthiest woman in town, had the front pew in the Congregational church.

But Arnold's father's finances failed, and the man proved to be a weakling when not buoyed up by credit. As long as the mother had money, creditors were patient with her husband, but now they closed in on him. He was much overextended, and he lost the business. Unable to endure failure, he soon became the town drunkard. Benedict, therefore, in his late teens was surrounded by an atmosphere of disgrace.

The church was kind to Mrs. Arnold and did not take away her pew when she was no longer able to pay for it, and she would march up to it every Sunday morning, dragging Benedict with her in his shabby clothes. The exposure filled him with rage and humiliation.

Benedict early joined the Continental Army, was wounded at Quebec, won a number of brilliant battles, and was one of the chief generals at the Battle of Saratoga.

In Philadelphia, Arnold apparently determined to build himself a fortress of wealth. He had seen how when wealth vanishes strong men are often struck down. When he was appointed to his Philadelphia post, he ordered a closing of all the shops, and by this stroke controlled all of the retail business. He demanded a cut in every enterprise that was going on, including, of course, the shipping traffic. In short, he owned a piece of certain ships. He also controlled the business of various wagon trains which supplied the city as well as the Continental Army on the outskirts of the city.

48

He certainly was demonstrating that money was his god and that his conscience could be easily appeased.

Peggy had also recently felt the humiliation and sting of near-poverty. Though the Shippens had been great persons in the city for several generations and still owned a handsome house there, Peggy's father proved to be a timid soul. He had never had to struggle to make a fortune, and as long as his prestige was bolstered by favorable circumstances, he was a fine gentleman of the community. But when the War for Independence broke out, he became frightened. He couldn't figure out which side was going to win, and he decided that he should not become committed either way. That left him with no employment from either side and obviously no certainty as to the future. The Continental paper money which he had was virtually valueless, and he had only a small store of British money which he felt must last out until the end of the war, whenever that might be.

He had always idealized Peggy and taken pride in her popularity and fine clothes. Now, prior to her engagement to Arnold, he began to croak incessantly about the lack of funds and to insist that they must cut down on expenses. Peggy should not spend anything on fancy dresses. Furthermore, she must be very careful about whom she entertained or with whom she went to dances. He felt that the social situation was very ticklish indeed and that the Shippens should be as inconspicuous as possible. The father's timidity was further increased by a committee of Quakers who called upon him, protesting that his daughters (Peggy had several sisters) should curb their conspicuous activities in attending many parties lest their behavior show a lack of patriotism. The Quakers were a powerful element in Philadelphia, and it would not be wise to affront them.

After Margaret's marriage to Arnold, she regained financial security, but she had had a chilling experience about what life might be like in poverty. Hence, she was conditioned to listen with interest about any proposals which might help her husband's future financial security. From the beginning, it seemed that André was the chief persuader, as evidence subsequently verified.

There have been several recent attempts to accept the statements of British officers affirming that Peggy Shippen had a part in inducing Arnold to betray West Point. An American writer in a recent article alleged that contemporary British officers, unidentified, had so alleged. Randolph G. Adams, writing in the *Dictionary of American Biography,* is more specific. He quotes a document, "in Clinton's own handwriting," which alleged that Arnold's wife "obtained for her services which was [*sic*] very meritorious, 350 pounds."

But why should Clinton be believed? Who gave this money to Peggy Shippen? Did Clinton personally? Was the sum given to André to pay to her? If there was such a sum, is there any evidence that it left André's pockets? The testimony of Clinton is suspect. As commander-in-chief of the British forces in America, he had been a colossal failure. The armies of Burgoyne and Cornwallis had been surrendered to the Americans. He, as commander-in-chief, had not prevented those disasters. His scheme for capturing West Point had been bungled by his own adjutant general. He had a motive for slandering others involved in his unhappy career.

After the marriage, Arnold had established himself and Peggy in a lavish home. That played into André's hands, because Arnold was accustoming himself to a fancy way of life which would require money to maintain indefinitely. When a man extends his scale of living, it is very difficult for him to cut back.

Arnold, meanwhile, was being persecuted by the Continental Congress, or at least he so regarded their nosing into his affairs. He was accused, with justice, of profiteering in many ways, though as long as George Washington protected him he did not need to be afraid. Washington regarded Arnold as a great military commander, and Washington also was being continually nagged at by the Continental Congress.

Washington's regard for Arnold was well based, for Arnold had endured great physical suffering occasioned by his bravery. His first wound was suffered during a siege of Quebec when a bullet entered his right leg below the knee and ripped all the way down to his heel. He had to be carried from the field, and the wound was a long time in healing. However, he was able to return to combat by the time of the Battle of Saratoga when Burgoyne was marching south, expecting to be able to cut off New England from the rest of the colonies. The British general had grossly underestimated both the number and the determination of the colonials. Also, he expected reinforcements from below which never arrived. At any rate, American General Horatio Gates did a brilliant job in planning the American strategy which led to the capture of Burgoyne's entire army. Arnold's dashing assault was an impressive part in the victory, though Gates never gave Arnold any credit for his part. Gates, in fact, was jealous of Arnold and resented his presence. Gates had valid grounds for his resentment. He knew that Burgoyne was far from his base of supplies and must fall into his hands with a minimum of fighting. Gates was in charge and Arnold had no right to alter the plans, but impatiently he led troops forward on his own authority. Arnold, dashed out into the open recklessly and came under British fire. His horse was shot from under him; he was thrown hard on the ground and broke the leg which had been wounded in the Quebec encounter. He was carried from the field, suffering great agony. At the American Army hospital in Albany the doctors told Arnold that his leg should be amputated. He protested that he would rather die than be a cripple, and demanded that they must fix him up some way and he would take the chance of gangrene's setting in. The doctors were able to save his leg, but he went with a bad limp for many months, and the wounded leg was ultimately shorter than his other one so that he had to wear a built-up shoe. All this is pertinent to Arnold's availability in Philadelphia where André could talk with him.

As André developed his proposal to Arnold it sounded persuasive. He held that the British Government was going to win the war anyhow; that if Arnold agreed to become a Loyalist and join the British forces £10,000 would be paid. Further, if he could deliver West Point the reward would be £20,000. In that case Arnold and Peggy could move to London, he would be a wealthy man, and the bestowal of a peerage would be almost certain. What a vision for the tempted Benedict: The Earl Arnold and his Countess Peggy!

There were certain wide gaps in the André scheme. First of all, one does not turn over a fortress as one might turn over a key to a garage. It would be necessary for British troops to infest the place and be allowed to do so gradually without arousing the suspicion of the American garrison. As a military genius Arnold could see that there were many points and plans that would have to be worked out carefully. André was disappointed to hear that, but he insisted that Arnold could manage to do the trick. Arnold also pointed out that he was not yet in charge of West Point, might not ever be. It was up to General Washington to determine that, though Arnold agreed he would apply to his commander for that post.

George Washington had other plans which came near ruining this whole scheme. He visited Arnold in a mood of enthusiasm, for he was about to confer a high honor. He told Arnold that a new campaign was in the cards, that he was going to place an entire division under Arnold's command, and that the prospects looked good for decisive victories that would bring the British to terms.

Arnold was dumfounded at this proposal, for his mind had already been seduced by dreams of wealth and a British peerage. Arnold, of course, showed himself a fool in worldly matters to have been carried away by such dreams, but André was persuasive and he was the adjutant under Clinton, presumably acting with his authority.

Arnold expressed his deep appreciation to General Washington but said that he was incapable of taking the field because of his wounded leg which was still extremely painful. He felt that a proper recognition, if Washington so desired to honor him, would be to be put in command of West Point. Washington said that commanding West Point was no job for a man with Arnold's dash and vigor; it was virtually a retirement post for some honorable old soldier who could just keep the fort in shape but would not be called upon for action. As to the bad leg, Arnold did not need to let that deter him. He could be carried into action in a wagon; his very name would fire the troops. His zeal, his military skill, his ability at organization, his coordination of all the facts which made for success in a campaign—all of those abilities Arnold had to the nth degree.

Arnold protested that he still was not well enough, that pain would dull the edge of his fighting spirit, that what he needed was more months to restore his physical state. He would be glad to give up his civilian work in Philadelphia and recuperate at West Point where at least he would be somewhat allied with the military campaign and certainly available for consultation. Washington was profoundly disappointed, but finally he agreed to Arnold's proposal and appointed him commander at West Point.

Arnold and Peggy, therefore, left their sumptuous home in Philadelphia and moved to West Point. The commandant did not make his home inside the fortress—but established a residence in the nearby countryside. There his wife lived and there he returned nightly.

Washington continued with his plan for a new campaign which involved land sorties near the west bank of the Hudson not far from West Point, and intermittently he visited Arnold's residence. This, of course, was an unforeseen and frightening development for Arnold.

A major question for Arnold was how to meet André without arousing suspicion. Arnold at this stage had an acute guilt complex. With his prestige he presumably could have summoned André to the fort and had a private conference with him there, but he tried to carry everything on without suspicion; this, of course, ultimately made the situation worse. Furthermore, he felt obliged to send certain messages to Clinton's headquarters through a go-between, referring to André by a pseudonym and trying to arrange a meeting at some neutral point out of sight of anybody. Ultimately there was an agreement that the meeting would take place at midnight in the woods near Arnold's residence.

The whole business had a preposterous melodramatic air which was probably pleasing to the theatrical instincts of André but was not regarded happily by Clinton. Clinton cautioned his adjutant general to be extremely careful, for example not to wear civilian clothes while carrying incriminatory papers; for if caught in that situation, he would be subject to treatment as a spy, whereas if in uniform he would have the status of an officer carrying *captured* papers, not to commit his office to anything that might prove embarrassing, and not to offer more than £6,000 as an original payment.

With some difficulty, Arnold and André found each other in the woods, where various differences developed. The opening conference was disturbing because the Britisher did not bring any cash down payment as Arnold had expected and now André's

54

best initial offer was £6,000 for preliminary activities. This, of course, was backtracking on the 10 and 20 proposal that had been spoken of previously. But then, Clinton had strongly told André that that sum was the best he could offer at the moment. Furthermore, Clinton had suggested that some more practical officer might better undertake the negotiations. André naturally objected to that because the whole scheme had been his brainchild. Clinton did not seem to realize that André expected that by having a principal part in this intrigue he would also receive great prestige and reward from the home government. Clinton, on the other hand, was dubious about the whole enterprise. He knew that Arnold had vast ability, was a favorite of General Washington, and was seemingly an unlikely prospect for the proposed plan. In fact, Clinton thought that the whole business might be some kind of a hoax. He feared trickery which might result in making him look ridiculous. He warned André not to go inside the Rebel lines.

Following the conference in the woods Arnold said that the necessary papers were at a house several miles away, a house occupied only by his agent, Smith. Smith was an eager and somewhat stupid fellow who had been acting as a go-between on profitable schemes for Arnold. There was trading back and forth between the British and the American lines as each needed products which could be supplied by the other. This was technically illegal but was winked at on both sides as an economic convenience. Smith had dealt with John Anderson, the pseudonym which André used, hence if Smith should be at home, as was probable, the presence of the newcomer would not arouse suspicion. Smith indeed would be proud to have knowledge that a secret conference was going on, and in fact he welcomed the appearance of the visitors.

Arnold and André retired to a room on the second floor where André removed his military coat. Smith walked into the room uninvited and stared with surprise at the British Army cloak which had been thrown across a chair. Arnold explained that Anderson was a Philadelphia merchant who had brought the cloak in case he should be stopped somewhere in British territory. That was hardly plausible, but Smith was so excited at being taken into this confidence that he accepted the story without question. At Arnold's suggestion Smith then withdrew and left the two principals alone.

Arnold had explained to André that it would not have been practical to take the various papers down to the woods as they could not read them without a lantern which might attract the attention of any passerby. He then produced a sheaf of papers which he had written without bothering to disguise his hand. These gave maps and full details about the location of various sections of the fort. As day was beginning to dawn he told André that it would be wise to wait until nighttime to attempt a return to the British lines and that Smith would stay to look after him.

Meanwhile Arnold said he would return to his residence, as an extended absence would appear peculiar. Hence, he left promptly and rode back to his house where he found Peggy in a somewhat quizzical mood. She rebuked him for staying out all night without letting her know in advance. She had been worried, and thought that he might be having a rendezvous with Smith, and these secret trips always gave her concern.

However, she was elated by the fact that General Washington and Lafayette were only a day or two's journey away and had sent word that they would like to stay overnight with the Arnolds or, if delayed, at least have breakfast with them. It was an honor, of course, to entertain the Chief, and the presence of Lafayette would be delightful, for the Frenchman was in his early twenties, was devoted to Peggy, and had great social charm.

Arnold was somewhat disturbed at Washington's coming so close. He would, of course, inspect West Point. Nevertheless, he doubtless would not linger for more than a day or two, and his mere presence would tend to give confidence to the staff of the fort that Arnold was a reliable officer in the American establishment.

While Arnold was enjoying these comfortable reflections, André was unhappily waiting for darkness to enable him to return to the British lines. Smith, as his guide, was proving to be an annoying nuisance. In the first place Smith insisted that André not wear his British cloak; instead Smith loaned him a handsome cloak of his own so that he was fully dressed in civilian clothes.

André by this act was violating Clinton's instructions. He had already violated the first instructions not to go inside the Rebel lines. The next change in plan by Smith was to go across the river by public ferry rather than by his own boat. Smith was not an expert oarsman, and he feared to cross the river where there had been intermittent firing from both sides. Hence they went down the line to King's Ferry, which was large enough to take their horses also. The crossing passed without incident, though André was perturbed at Smith's habit of chatting with various American officers of his acquaintance.

Once they had reached the east shore of the Hudson the plan was to proceed on land until they arrived at the British lines some twenty miles to the south. André was in a fever of impatience to keep moving, but Smith was in no hurry because he was enjoying his importance. The result was that he made continuous excuses for delaying the journey, stopping for meals, on another occasion stopping overnight. Two or three days elapsed after they had left the conference house. Ultimately, however, they came to a bridge which marked the beginning of territory held by the British. André thanked Smith and told him to return to the American side. Both Smith and André had passes signed by Arnold which supposedly would protect them if accosted by any sentry. André now was in high spirits as he galloped along the road. He was still fifteen miles from the actual British headquarters, but this was known to be Loyalist territory and he had no fears. There were only a few houses and few passersby. He had no reason to expect being molested.

However, suddenly he came upon three civilians. The tallest grabbed the horse's bridle and demanded who André was and where he was going. He said, "Who are you, Loyalists or Rebels?" They made some equivocal answer and André said, "I am a British officer on urgent business and cannot be delayed." They replied that they wanted to know more about that and wondered why he was wearing civilian clothes. He said that these men would be in trouble if they tried to delay him. They then confessed that they were Rebels. Then André said, "Well, in that case I have this pass from General Arnold. Now let me go."

The oldest man of the three, whose name was Paulding and who was the only one able to read, said, "Oh-ho, you first said that you were a British officer and now you say that you are on an errand for Arnold. We think that you may be a spy. Get down off that horse while we search you."

André was obliged to comply. The three men took him to a field which lay behind a thicket and was hidden from the road. They made him first strip above the waist while they went through his clothes eagerly, but they found nothing but his gold watch and some Continental currency which he had borrowed from Smith. Then they made him strip down to his boots and stockings. This was an appalling delay and an insult to André, but his gifts as an actor were helpful. He regarded the event as a piece of melodrama which would make interesting conversation later on.

Even though André was now almost naked he was not uncomfortable, because it was mid-September and the weather was still warm. Paulding, the ringleader, said, "Well, let's see what are in his boots and stockings." They took off one boot and stocking and found nothing. Then they took off the other, and inside that stocking were the papers which Arnold had provided.

Paulding read them with growing interest but without the education to comprehend their full significance. However, he said that these were Arnold's papers all right and they would take this fellow back to Arnold. André was inwardly vastly relieved, for of course, a return to Arnold was the safest thing that could happen to him.

André was still known to his captors by his pseudonym, John Anderson, and that deceit was maintained in the papers which had been taken from him and did not have any immediate bearing as far as he might imagine. His three captors had been augmented by several more, and André rather enjoyed the drama of the parade even though his arms had been tied behind him. The road which the captors now used was a trifle inland from the one which André and Smith had traveled. It led to a Rebel post in charge of Lt. Col. John Jameson. The latter read the documents which had been seized and had the background which Paulding had lacked to comprehend their significance. He could hardly believe his eyes. He was the first American to have any knowledge or suspicion of Arnold's treason. In fact, he thought there must be some explanation. He dared not delay taking André to Arnold, as Arnold was the ranking authority in the region. Yet Jameson worried. Suppose Arnold proved to be a traitor and Jameson neglected to notify the commander-in-chief, who was within a day's ride. Jameson decided to take the chance of sending the papers on to General Washington, who at this time was near Danbury, Connecticut. All this, of course, was unknown to the so-called John Anderson.

Washington, meanwhile, was having an encouraging journey. The whole countryside was clearly loyal to the American cause. Also, the general's companions were in a cheerful mood after the grim days of Valley Forge. The young Lafayette, who had been made a major-general by the Continental Congress, felt that victory would soon be in sight. A companion who had come from France with him, Stephen Tourison, was another enthusiast for the American cause. In fact, Tourison did not return to France, but married an American girl in Philadelphia and established a family in this country. Tourison had been born in 1756 in France and was a year older than Lafayette. A valiant Revolutionary, he endured the winter at Valley Forge and fought at the Battle of Brandywine. His Philadelphia wife was one of a colony of French emigrés who had settled in Philadelphia after having been driven out of Nova Scotia. All of Tourison's emotional ties obviously were to America.

The whole party were looking forward to the forthcoming visit at the Arnold residence. Lafayette and Washington would sit at the head table with Benedict and Peggy, but there would be adequate accommodations for the entire staff.

While all these plans were going forward, the principals, unknown to themselves, were on the verge of drama. Arnold could not understand why he had had no word from André. André wished that his captors would hurry up and deliver him to Arnold. Washington was taking a leisurely course on his inspection trip of various fortifications while Lafayette was eagerly anxious to get ready for their social visit. In fact, early in the morning of September 25 he urged upon Washington that they were expected for breakfast at the Arnolds' home and shouldn't permit a delay. Washington smilingly said that he knew that most of his young officers were in love with Mrs. Arnold and that they should not keep her waiting. However, he detailed two lieutenants to speed to the Arnold home and urge their hosts not to delay breakfast.

This was done. Arnold sat down to breakfast with his two new guests and urged them to begin eating until Peggy came down. He himself attempted to eat but paced about intermittently. As he walked into the pantry a lieutenant and aide came rushing into the house saying that General Washington and staff were a short distance away. Furthermore, a certain John Anderson had been captured with incriminating papers which were in the hands of Washington. Arnold thanked the messenger, trying to preserve an outward calm. Then he rushed up to the bedroom, said to Peggy, "All is lost," fled downstairs, mounted a horse, commandeered a barge, and had the crew convey him to the British warship *Vulture,* which was downstream on the east bank of the Hudson.

Meanwhile, Washington arrived with Lafayette and party in a state of great agitation. A witness says that his hands trembled as he said to Lafayette in a shaking voice, "Arnold has betrayed us. Now whom can we trust?" He did not send a pursuit after Arnold, possibly thinking that it was all too sickening. Arnold had been one of his dearest friends. He did not think of any plan for capturing the man or what to do with him if they could capture him behind the British lines. Washington's job was to pursue the war and to face whatever circumstances might develop. What should they do about this man Anderson? He should be hanged as a spy, but perhaps there were more traitors, and it might be well to temporize with Anderson for the time being to see if they could get some more information out of him. Very shortly, Washington received a communication from the spy himself, who, of course, was being held in custody by the Rebels.

Anderson wrote with unparalleled brass, which was inherent in his nature, that he should explain his mission, which had been discovered. He stated that he was Major André, an officer in His Majesty's service, and that he was entitled to all military courtesies. He acknowledged that he had had dealings with Arnold within the American lines, but under the protection of a flag of truce.

André also had a threat which he hoped might be effective.

He wrote that the British were holding three important South Carolina prisoners, who could be executed but might be exchanged for him.

Washington was not impressed. A commissioned officer who turns spy must take the risks of his new role, if caught. The plea of a flag of truce was completely specious. The flag of truce cannot be invoked as a cover for a spy. However, General Clinton moved into the situation ardently, trying to persuade Washington to some kind of arrangement that would spare André. Washington continued to delay making an immediate decision, apparently thinking that time might turn up some wide ramifications of the plot.

Meanwhile, Arnold had been added to Clinton's official staff. He had been assigned to one or two minor engagements against the colonials, in the hope that some of his previous fellow officers might turn to the British cause. Arnold himself had said that once he turned, many would follow him. He probably believed that, but it proved not to be the case. Only twenty-eight persons joined him. The zeal of most of the colonists for independence was unshakable.

When the surrender to Cornwallis at Yorktown ended the British hopes in America, Arnold fled to England and Peggy followed him there.

The British had no reason to be self-righteous in denouncing a turncoat. There had been many many such instances in England's varied history, and no shame attached to being a turncoat if successful. That was the rub. Arnold's program had failed, and the failure had made Britain look inept and foolish. The home government gave him asylum but no rewards. He and Peggy lived for several years in England while he carried on an export and import business with varying success. Socially, he and his wife died in virtual isolation, and their passing created no stir.

As André continued still alive in his place of captivity his hopes gradually deteriorated. It became clear that he was not going to be exchanged for other prisoners, and there was something mysterious in the fact that there was delay in disposing of his case. The one cheerful element in his situation was that the young Alexander Hamilton was put in charge of him. Hamilton was very close to Washington and, like André, was foreign-born, not one of the tough New Englanders who had been raised with ideas of colonial independence. André played on the fact that Hamilton was a man of the world, and that flattery worked. Hamilton found his prisoner fascinating and continually pleaded his cause with Washington. While the commander-in-chief had no intention of releasing the prisoner, at least Hamilton felt that the prisoner should have the soldier's privilege of being shot and not the disgrace of being hanged as a spy.

As the capture of André became more widely known, however, the public increasingly recalled the fate of Nathan Hale. When Hale had been hanged, every insulting circumstance had been heaped upon him. He had been refused a Bible; he had been denied the comfort of a chaplain; he had been left hanging for several days as an example; his body had been buried in an unmarked grave. His family had erected a memorial tombstone to him in the cemetery at Coventry, but the actual location of the body was unknown. The very fact that Hale was hanged and without trial or delay had been widely resented throughout the colonies, and as these gratuitous insults had become known the bitterness ran deep. Visitors to André began to mention the fate of Nathan Hale. The frequency of such comments began to annoy André and doubtless frightened him. He protested to one visitor that he trusted that no one saw a parallel beween his case and that of Hale. He was an adjutant general on the staff of the British commanding officer, whereas Hale was only a young schoolteacher. André did not comprehend the fact that the teacher and the local minister, often the same man, were the most respected persons in any village. New England had a high regard for learning. While farming was the chief occupation, many a farmer was better educated than the town merchant, and many held college degrees.

André was not only second in rank on Clinton's staff but also held the commission of major. Hale, on the other hand, was only a captain, and only a captain in Washington's army, which had no status at all in British opinion.

It was almost impossible for André to adjust to the environment in which he found himself a prisoner of these uncouth persons. His days in Philadelphia over the past several years had been so delightful. He had been a favorite of the ladies—the Loyalists, the declared Rebels, and the undeclared. He had been received favorably by the popular Margaret Shippen and had given her a lock of his hair. Yet now there was talk of his being hanged. In fact, if General Washington did not take action there was a real possibility of his being lynched.

In spite of pleas by General Clinton, Washington finally set aside the day for the hanging of Major André on an open plain. A gallows was erected, and a large group of colonials gathered around. In those days a hanging was supposed to be a public entertainment, and of course in this situation it was a very unusual one.

Hundreds of persons were there. André was asked if he would like to have a chaplain, but he said no. If he was an instrument of the devil as many seemed to believe, certainly a chaplain might seem to be inappropriate. At any rate he came to the gallows. The procedure was that the victim climbed aboard a wagon and had the noose put around his neck. Then at a given signal the wagon moved away and the victim was left hanging.

André climbed aboard the wagon, still interested in doing dramatics. He waved the hangman aside and put the noose over his neck himself. Then he said some theatrical words to the effect that he was about to die in good conscience and that he trusted he would be remembered favorably. The crowd was not sympathetic. The signal was given, the wagon pulled out, and within a short time Major André was hanged until he was dead.

The body was deposited in a grave not far from the foot of the gallows among others of those who had been hanged. The field was in the town of Tappan, New York. Although the area was actively farmed, the farmers avoided plowing near the graves. Accordingly, the remains of André were left undisturbed for forty years until some British administration requested that they be disinterred and sent to England.

The immediate news of André's hanging created profound embarassment in the Tory Cabinet. One did not hang a British officer, still less a deputy adjutant general representing the British commander-in-chief in America. Some means must be undertaken to wipe out that disgrace, to build up the character of André into a hero. Hence it was decided to erect a monument to his memory in Westminster Abbey. The wording on it referred to him as a hero who had given his life for King and country.

CHAPTER VII

John Paul Jones

Founder of American Sea Power

Not every youth participating in the Revolution was activated by love of his homeland or by the ideal of independence.

Some were basically adventurers and moved by dreams of glory. Such a one was John Paul Jones, the dashing hero of the Continental Navy. His numerous victories on the high seas made him famous in the annals of American history. Even partisan British accounts give him credit for ingenuity and daring. Britain, of course, was famous as a leading sea power after the defeat of the Spanish Armada, and the love of the sea was deeply implanted in the British consciousness.

John Paul Jones was born in 1747; therefore, he was in his late twenties when he became attached to the American cause. He was not a colonist by birth, for he was born in Scotland under the name of John Paul. He adopted the name Jones after he had left Scotland and moved to America because he had been accused of killing a crew member on one of his ships. Ultimately he was exonerated, but for a time he apparently felt the need of concealing his identity.

But to return to his life in Scotland: After spending a short period at the parish school in Kirkbean, Scotland, at the age of twelve he left home and entered into the service of a shipowner in the port of Whitehaven, England, where he served as an apprentice. On his first voyage he came to Fredericksburg, Virginia, where an elder brother was working as a tailor. He stayed in this colony for some days and improved his time by studying navigation. When his employer failed in business the young fellow soon got a job on a slave ship as third mate. At the age of nineteen he was first mate on another slave ship, and by the age of twenty-seven he had become a captain of another vessel.

John Paul Jones realized that there was no future, certainly no glory, in continuing in the slave trade, and when the American Revolution broke out he saw an opportunity to achieve distinction in those troubled waters. His brother died, leaving him a modest inheritance, and Jones moved to Philadelphia with the purpose of cultivating influential leaders in the Continental Congress.

He was only partly successful in this enterprise, as the men in the Congress were not particularly receptive to new persons and new ideas. They seemed to be constitutionally jealous of the active persons who were actually carrying on the struggle. Their quarrels with General Washington, for example, are well known. Jones desired to be an admiral for the new Continental Navy, but Congress was willing only to make him a lieutenant. With that modest title he was the first ranking officer and the first individual to command a ship flying the Continental flag.

Jones, however, was persistent and persuasive. He soon made the acquaintance of Joseph Hewes, delegate from North Carolina. and of banker Robert Morris. Hewes was a powerful advocate of naval warfare, and Morris was an important figure in the councils of the Congress. With the backing of those two men Jones was in a strong political position and could not be dislodged from a leadership which he was able to handle with great distinction.

Jones' first conspicuous voyage was in 1776 when he was promoted to be captain of a vessel named the *Providence*. His tour with that vessel was prophetic of his future career. The *Providence* destroyed British shipping domination and took sixteen prizes, including a transport laden with soldiers' clothing, a highly important capture for the Continental Army, which was short of all sorts of supplies. The *Providence* also captured a privateer of ten guns. In these engagements Jones had displayed a rare gift for speed and strategy.

His next significant move was to establish a base in France. France was sympathetic to the American cause but even more motivated by an enmity toward England. Hence Jones was allowed to establish his base at Brest. This was a material advantage compared with operating out of any colonial port. Brest was near to the main Atlantic seaways, which were continually plied with British vessels. Jones was helped not only by his own skill but by the fact that British seamanship was at a low ebb.
Lord Sandwich, head of the Admiralty, was an incompetent politician, interested primarily in his own importance in the Cabinet and incapable of building an efficient navy.

In an early voyage out of Brest, Jones had the particular satisfaction of sailing into the harbor of Whitehaven, where he had started his sea career about a decade earlier. This time he was commanding the *Ranger,* a larger vessel than the *Providence*. He sailed into the harbor of Whitehaven; from his ship he spiked the defending guns of the harbor and was able to mingle freely among the British ships, hoping to destroy them all. At the outset he was unsuccessful because of the difficulty of maneuvering.

He sailed around in the area for twenty-eight days, however, and fought a one-hour battle with the British vessel *Drake,* which ended in the surrender of the latter. That victory caused a great sensation in the maritime world. The *Drake* had been regarded as a capable fighting ship, but it was on the defensive throughout against Jones' superior strategy. During this twenty-eight day expedition Jones captured seven vessels and completely terrified the whole English coast.

When he returned to France he was received as a great popular hero. The French themselves had never been efficient seamen, and they had been galled at the longtime success of the British in blockading their ports virtually at will. Now suddenly a new young nation had developed a prowess that could hold the British lion in check.

The French minister of marine and Benjamin Franklin, who was the American ambassador to France, each recognized Jones as an outstanding hero in the American cause. France put under his command a retired East India ship of forty guns which was reoutfitted at the expense of the French Government. Jones renamed it the *Bonhomme Richard* in honor of Franklin (Franklin had fame as a writer under the penname Poor Richard).

Big events were in the air. A proposal was drawn up whereby Jones and Lafayette would make a joint attack on England: Jones to carry the naval part and to land troops in England under the command of Lafayette. This ambitious program, however, was wisely abandoned. The possibility of defeating the British on their own soil was remote.

However, the *Bonhomme Richard* did set forth with a small flotilla and encountered a British fleet in the Baltic Sea. A general engagement did not ensue, but the British vessel *Serapis* attacked the *Bonhomme Richard*. Apparently each fleet was prepared to let the engagement be decided by its flagship. The *Serapis* was a two-decker and had larger guns than the *Bonhomme Richard*. Its superior strength seemed to assure a victory. Jones had to do something to offset that advantage. He ran his vessel alongside

69

the *Serapis* and lashed the two ships together, bow and stern, so that their cannon were muzzle to muzzle and not usable. Jones had the superior manpower and hoped to conquer by his musketry. The battle lasted for three hours. Each ship was damaged from time to time by the outbreak of fire. Finally the *Serapis* struck its colors and the *Bonhomme Richard* was able to sail away the victor.

The encounter was a dubious triumph because the *Bonhomme Richard* had been kept afloat during the battle only by continuous use of its pumps. Moreover, its injuries were so serious that on the second day after the encounter the vessel sank and Jones transferred his command to another ship, the *Alliance*.

Furthermore, he was not able to make his way back to France but limped into port of Texel in Holland, with his squadron and the prizes they had captured.

Holland was neutral and promptly was requested by the British ambassador to treat Jones as a criminal, describing him as "a rebel subject, a pirate, and a criminal of the state." Holland did not turn over the Jones prizes, for the French Government stepped in, affirming that these properties belonged to it. Jones personally, however, was expelled from Holland, being allowed only to command the *Alliance*. He was able to elude the British vessels waiting for him and returned to the coast of France.

From France he ultimately sailed for America in 1781, arriving at Philadelphia after having been absent from America nearly four years. By this time Congress received him with considerable honor. He submitted his personal accounts, showing that he had not received a dollar of pay for his five years of service. After the war, which virtually ended with the surrender of Cornwallis, Jones devoted himself primarily to the writing of naval history.

The judgment of Britain on this man was an interesting revelation of the British psychology. The British *Dictionary of National*

Biography could not help but admire Jones' maritime achievements but it still regarded him as a traitor. It said,

> Jones was a man of distinguished talent and originality, a thorough seaman, and of the most determined and tenacious courage. His faults were due to defective training. Excessive vanity, and a desire for "glory," which was, as he wrote, "infinite," and recognized no obstacles, made him a traitor to his country [meaning Britain], and it made him quarrelsome, mean and selfish.

CHAPTER VIII

Lafayette

The Young Allies

Lafayette was a teen-age French Patriot who became a brilliant soldier on the staff of General Washington.

His full name was Marie Joseph Paul Yves Roch Gilbert du Motier, Marquis de Lafayette. That string of names represented various aristocratic families in his ancestry. He was born into one of the leading families of France in September, 1757, and subsequently married into another leading family, so that in some respects fortune favored him. It was not necessary for him to risk his life for a cause, but he frankly was a romanticist who sought for glory. As he told Washington and others, he sought *la gloire*.

He came from a line of military men, and from earliest days expected that the Army would be his career. When Lafayette was only two years old, his father was killed at the Battle of Minden in Germany, where the enemy was a combination of German and British soldiers. Lafayette throughout his life was anti-British, in particular because of his father's death, but also because the British had conquered Canada from the French during the Seven Years' War.

His mother died when he was only thirteen years old, and her father soon after, leaving his fortune to the young boy. This provided an income of 120,000 *livres* annually. The records differ on what that would mean in modern currency, but it was possibly $12,000. At any rate, it was a sum which enabled him to live handsomely and associate in the top levels of court society. The young man, however, was not continuously happy. Like many a teen-ager, he suffered occasions of agonized embarrassment. One time when he was at the court, he had too much to drink and danced so awkwardly that Marie Antoinette, the Queen, openly laughed at him.

As he grew older, he enlisted in the French Army and went to camp at Metz, but did not see combat service. He was mentally active and read much of Rousseau and other writers of the period. He made frequent visits to Paris and Versailles, participating in the social life of the era and becoming acquainted with persons of prominence from different countries. One of these visitors was the Duke of Gloucester, a brother of the British King. Gloucester was sympathetic with the love of freedom which was very much in the air and told Lafayette that he agreed with the protests of the American colonies who were resenting various of the measures imposed on them by the British Government. This was one of the earliest impressions made on Lafayette, and it turned his thoughts toward America as a possible field where he might fight for a noble cause and achieve glory. He sought out the American ambassador at Paris and discussed the possibilities, but no immediate plans were made.

At seventeen he married a daughter of the de Noailles family. This family was eminent politically and socially. As was frequently the case, the marriage had been arranged by the parents when the principal parties were children. That was a customary procedure among aristocratic families—somewhat shocking to romantic

American notions, yet often successful. It provided a marriage between persons of similar background, family customs, and beliefs. Such marriages were usually permanent, and not afflicted by the frequent divorce rate which has occurred on the American scene. However, that type of prearrangement is feasible only in a stabilized society where the same families continue for generation after generation. In the case of Lafayette, the marriage was successful, enduring for life.

Marriage, however, did not interfere with a man's career, and a soldier in particular was expected to go wherever destiny might take him. By the time he was nineteen, Lafayette had made up his mind to offer his services to the American colonies, who had already declared their independence. He conferred with Silas Deane, the American ambassador, and through a friend arranged for the purchase of a vessel on which Lafayette sailed for America in April, 1777. Deane had promised him a commission in the Continental Army.

He arrived at Georgetown, South Carolina, where he was entertained by a friend, Maj. Benjamin Huger, a name whose pronunciation the Americans anglicized to "Hewgee." It was logical for Lafayette to land initially in South Carolina because there was a sizable French colony in Charleston. The French had established a Huguenot church, which they supported financially even though each citizen was taxed to support the Church of England. The Hugers were a large clan, and several of them were already in the Continental Army. Lafayette finally moved on to Philadelphia, a journey which took him six weeks. There he was coldly received by the Continental Congress, and his commission from Deane was ignored. The Congress had seen a number of foreign fortune-hunters, most of whom were seeking general's commissions, and many were not qualified for such responsibility.

Lafayette addressed a letter to the Congress. He wrote that he would pay his own way and would enlist as a volunteer. That mollified their attitude, and he was introduced to General Washington. Washington took an immediate fancy to him and added him to his staff. Lafayette soon saw combat service and fought at the Battle of Brandywine, where he was wounded in the leg. That injury established his acceptability with the American troops. Here was an ally who was an actual fighting man, not just someone seeking a soft staff job.

The wound was sufficiently serious so that he was moved to Bethlehem, Pennsylvania, to recuperate. Bethlehem was founded by the Moravian Church, a sect which was pacifistic in its belief. It declined to fight with the Continental Army but was sympathetic to the cause and maintained a hospital throughout the war which cared for wounded Continental soldiers. When Lafayette returned to the Army, the attitude of Congress had changed, for they were convinced of his sincerity. He was commissioned a major general, in command of a regiment of Virginia light troops. These men spent the winter of 1778 at Valley Forge. Lafayette's youthfulness and his willingness to share the hardships of that winter made him highly popular. Before spring came, the Board of War authorized him to command an expedition for the conquest of Canada. This appealed to him immensely. He had visions of reclaiming Canada for France. That would be glory indeed! When he arrived at Albany, expecting to find an army of trained colonials all ready to undertake this mission, he found nothing. No preparations had been made, nothing planned. This neglect was never explained. He wrote to Washington in rage and humiliation, but apparently the expedition had never been a part of the commander's strategy—in fact, he may never have heard of it.

The tension, however, was relieved by the news that France had officially declared herself an American ally. This lifted the hopes of the American cause. It meant financial aid, supplies, and most importantly the assistance of French military aid. One unit arrived at Newport, Rhode Island, under General Rochambeau. Lafayette endeavored to persuade the general to make an attack on the British forces in the area, but Rochambeau was not willing to risk such an expedition at once. Apparently, his visit was meant to be chiefly a gesture of support.

Subsequently, Lafayette went on furlough and visited Boston, where he was greeted with great enthusiasm and was entertained at the home of Hancock.

By 1780, the American prospects looked much better. A new French fleet unit under de Grasse sailed for America, destined to blockade the port at Yorktown, Virginia. Meanwhile, Cornwallis had had only mediocre success in his Southern campaign, where he had hoped to destroy the Continental troops under General Greene. However, cavalry troops under Light Horse Harry Lee and the successful maneuvering of Greene had prevented any conclusive victory. Cornwallis had been handicapped by the fatal superiority complex which had hampered Great Britain throughout the war. Cornwallis was a peer of the Realm. He couldn't believe that these colonials, these commoners, could stand up against him indefinitely. He gradually abandoned his expeditions in the deep South and worked his way up into Virginia. While there, he heard of the successes of Lafayette, but he observed contemptuously, "The boy cannot escape me."

In due course—by this time it was 1781—he moved his army down to the Yorktown Peninsula, where he expected relief from the British Fleet, but de Grasse got to the harbor first!

The way out by land was blocked by a sizable concentration of the Continental Army. Cornwallis was cut off from supplies, and he had the option of being starved out or surrendering peacefully. He chose the latter course and led his troops to surrender

76

as prisoners of war while the band played "The World Turned Upside Down."

Lafayette was present at the scene and commented, "The play is over, the fifth act has just ended."

Lafayette had had his full taste of glory.

CHAPTER IX

James Madison

A Militant Patriot

A Voice against the Tories
by James Madison
(when an undergraduate)

Come noble Whigs, disdain these sons
Of screech owls, monkeys and baboons.
Keep up your minds to humorous themes
And verdant meads and flowing streams
Until this tribe of dunces find
The baseness of their groveling mind
And skulk within their dens together
Where each one's stench will kill his brother.

NEXT to Alexander Hamilton and Lafayette, probably the most famous youth of Revolutionary days was James Madison.

He entered the College of New Jersey (now Princeton) at the age of eighteen in 1769, was graduated in 1771, and took a year's graduate work. He lived in Nassau Hall for the entire period.

Madison became famous as the primary author* of the Federalist Papers, and of course as a President of the United States. Even in his late teens his mind was conspicuously able, and the College of New Jersey provided an exercise ground for it. Discussion was encouraged. The three underclasses declaimed weekly on the platform, sometimes with their own compositions, and sometimes repeating select pieces from Cicero, Shakespeare, and other famous authors.

The seniors had regular debates, some in Latin and some in English. Different subjects were discussed during the week, where two or three issues might be examined. The piety of the Sabbath was maintained by scheduling religious topics for debate on that day.

Madison was a mental genius with a mind of extraordinary clarity, but he had a weak constitution which made it impossible for him to carry out physical action. However, he compensated for this by being an expert in rifle marksmanship and in planning military strategy.

Madison was an oddball who suffered the agonies of adolescence. He was introverted and self-conscious. At one time he fell into melancholy and thought that he was not long to live but soon would be enjoying eternity. During those months, he found it difficult to concentrate on any work at all because he felt life was so transient.

---

* The Federalist Papers which appeared serially in the New York press were written by Madison, Alexander Hamilton, and John Jay. The precise authorship of some of the papers is unknown. Some were the joint work of Madison and Hamilton. Hamilton put together the first collected edition, containing an introduction and table of contents, hence he is regarded in some quarters as the primary author. Conversely Madison has been looked upon as the basic philosopher. Professor Edward Mead Earle of the Institute of Advanced Studies, Princeton, New Jersey, writes that Madison's "influence was so great that he might legitimately be called 'the master-builder of the Constitution'" (*The Federalist,* Modern Library edition).

Like many another young person, he became disillusioned with the church. He had been an ardent member of the Church of England but had come to resent the arbitrariness of its hierarchy. He denounced the denomination as coercive, hypocritical, and intolerant, and in a letter to a friend referred to "that diabolical hell-conceived principle of persecution which rages among some." He favored the disestablishment of the Anglican Church in Virginia, and by contrast, he referred to the liberality of the Protestant sects in Pennsylvania.

Madison's active mind thrived on revolutionary principles. The instruction at the College of New Jersey encouraged originality of thought. One of Madison's chief teachers, only twenty-five years old in 1769, was Ebenezer Pemberton, who was a famous classicist and lived to the age of ninety. Naturally for years he was regarded as an elder statesman, but he was a young man when he was a tutor of Madison.

Another teacher was Tapping Reeve, who later founded the Litchfield (Connecticut) Law School.

An interesting phase of Madison's student life was the sympathy of the undergraduates and the administration toward each other. The tyrannical attitude of the Tory government in England, coupled with that of the King, who sought "obedience" from his subjects, served to unite the administration and the students in self-protection. Madison's notebooks were full of complimentary remarks about his instructors. He referred to one as "remarkable for a skill in the sophomore studies." Another he described as an expert classicist and "a teacher of the most admirable scholarly and personal qualities."

An influential professor was William Churchill Houston, a member of various revolutionary bodies in New Jersey prior to 1776, who became a member of the Continental Congress and of local Rebel assemblies.

Madison's natural bent toward independence was fostered in his postgraduate days when John Witherspoon had arrived and become president of the college. Witherspoon was a champion of independence from his arrival in this country. Scotland nominally had been united with England, but the ancient rivalry persisted, and Witherspoon from the outset advocated that the colonies be separated from Great Britain.

Madison, though evidently a mental genius, was a typical undergraduate in the usual student routine. He was always short of funds. In one of his letter's home he said that with all his "frugality" he had not been able to meet the expenses "consistent with my staying here to the best advantage." Apparently the family sent him some more money, for at any rate he was able to stay in college.

All circumstances conspired to make Madison a young Revolutionary, though probably the chief influence was his own temperament, because his college activities and close friends in his class were of Revolutionary bent. He was an early member of the American Whig Society, which even then was active on campus. His classmates included Charles McKnight and Samuel Spring, who fought in the Revolution; also William Bradford, who became Attorney-General of the new country after independence had been achieved. Numerous other classmates were pioneers in the Revolution.

Madison and most of his classmates formed the core of Revolutionary leadership in New Jersey, and all of them, mostly still in their twenties, became organizing figures in the new Republic.

Madison was continually dissatisfied with the imperfections of existing institutions, a factor again characteristic of his years. He is an example of the fact that the odd ball of today may emerge as the genius of tomorrow.

As is characteristic of many a young person who revolts against

81

the church, Madison was deeply religious. He commented on Samuel Clarke's *A Discourse Concerning the Being and Attributes of God,* as follows:

> the belief in a God All Powerful wise and good, is so essential to the moral order of the World and to the happiness of man, that arguments which enforce it cannot be drawn from too many sources nor adapted with too much solicitude to the different characters and capacities to be impressed with it.

While in college, he kept track of events which were occurring in England and received numerous pamphlets from abroad. The fact that he kept in touch with the politics of the time is evidenced by a letter which he wrote to his father in 1770, saying:

> We have no public news but the base conduct of the merchants in New York, in breaking through their spirited resolutions not to import, a distinct account of which, I suppose, will be in the Virginia Gazette before this arrives. Their letter to the merchants in Philadelphia, requesting their concurrence, was lately burnt by the students of this place in the college yard, all of them appearing in their black gowns, and the bell tolling—The number of students has increased very much of late. There are about a hundred and fifteen in college and the grammar school, (twenty-two commence this fall,) all of them in American cloth.

In his after-college years, Madison dropped some of his cloistered attitude and sought to take arms for the colonies, but his genius still was directed toward the philosophy and construction of the new country.

CHAPTER X

Light-Horse Harry Lee

Chief of the Cavalry

THE most famous cavalryman in the Revolution was Henry Lee. He was also the youngest, and perhaps the wealthiest. He entered the College of New Jersey (Princeton) at the age of fourteen, accompanied by his brother Charles and a neighbor, James Madison. He completed the course in three years, which was then the standard schedule, and was looking forward to spending about two years abroad, studying law at the Middle Temple. He then expected to return home and handle the legal affairs of his vast family connections.

Lee was a part of the "FFV"—First Families of Virginia. These included a large Lee cousinhood, plus the Fairfaxes, the Blands, the Washingtons, and other leading names in the province. His mother had been Miss Lucy Grymes, once a sweetheart of the young George Washington. Her marriage to someone else did not break up their friendship. In fact, over the years Martha Washington became one of Lucy Lee's best friends.

Lee's parents lived on a huge estate which was organized like a feudal enterprise in England. In short, it was largely self-containing. It not only produced most of the grain, vegetables, fruit, meat, and fish that were needed but had the necessary services of a village economy. Mrs. Lee employed a cobbler, a tailor, a dressmaker, carpenters, and cabinetmakers. When her oldest son, Henry, was born, she bought two slaves to look after him. The big establishment used scores of slaves for its operations in the fields and the household.

Ultimately the advent of industrial machinery altered the economy of the countryside, and the famous Robert E. Lee, son of Henry, freed his slaves before the Civil War made slaves an issue.

The leading Virginia families considered themselves an aristocracy and felt a sense of *noblesse oblige.* Idleness was discouraged, and every man was supposed to carry his share of responsibility, whether in soldiering, in administering the properties, or in the professions. When Henry was only three, his father put him on a horse. He seemed to take to horsemanship instinctively and in no time at all could ride in the saddle or bareback. He also became a good judge of horseflesh, and by the time he organized his cavalry troop, he passed upon the quality of the animals selected as well as the riders.

The British Tory establishment, who looked down upon the tradesmen and other dissenters in Massachusetts, made a woeful mistake in their judgment of Virginians. They assumed that because the Virginians were rich they would also be conservative, and conservatism to them meant unquestioned loyalty to the King and the British establishment. Initially Virginians did support the monarchy and conservatism in politics, but their basic training was in self-rule. They had learned to manage their own affairs, and repeated interference from across the Atlantic did not sit well. George Washington, in his earlier days, was a moderate and repeatedly petitioned the Crown for redress of grievances, but these petitions generally went unanswered—in fact were regarded as a nuisance, perhaps as impertinence, coming from colonials.

By the time Henry was ready for college in 1770 his parents had decided that the College of New Jersey (Princeton) was a proper school for his education. Patrick Henry, authorized by the Virginia Burgesses, had started Committees of Correspondence between the various colonies, which soon resulted in the First Continental Congress.

It was in the background of this atmosphere of unrest that Henry entered the College of New Jersey. He was already sharp mentally. He had been tutored in Latin, so that he could speak it fluently as a young boy. He was also familiar with English writers, such as Pope, and was well grounded in English history. Later he became so famous as a cavalryman that his early capabilities as a scholar were overlooked.

At the College of New Jersey he found the competition of able minds of men who, like himself, came from distinguished families. As a freshman he found himself no longer the princeling of his family estate, but merely one among many. The College of New Jersey could only be attended by the well-to-do because of the expense. When Henry Lee entered, there were one hundred boys. Nassau Hall, one of the largest buildings in the colonies, was able to accommodate all of the undergraduates in sleeping quarters and dining rooms and in addition to provide classrooms and an assembly room.

Discipline was rigid and the schedule strenuous. The principal was Witherspoon, an imported Scotch dominie, who was a perfectionist and had no toleration for sloppy work. If a boy did not keep up with his studies, he was sent home, and there was no recourse.

The day began at five o'clock in the morning, when the president walked down the dormitory aisles, ringing a large bell. He had with him some stalwart assistants, and any boy who did not rise immediately was thrown out of bed. At five thirty, there was a half hour of prayer, with a brief sermon. From six to eight, there was study hour in the library. Not until eight did the students get their breakfast of meat and fish with tea or coffee as beverage.

From nine o'clock until one, there were classes in languages, moral philosophy, physical sciences, and composition. Henry enjoyed tackling strenuous mental challenges such as comparing Pope's translation of the *Odyssey* with the original and memorizing the poems of Milton. He had little admiration for the works of Shakespeare, which perhaps seemed too frivolous for his serious young mind.

At one o'clock came the midday meal, the most hearty of the day, which included meat, fish, bread, potatoes, and vegetables, washed down with beer or hard cider. No distilled liquor was allowed, but the seniors could drink ale. The boys had free time until three o'clock. Then there were afternoon recitations, after which everyone dressed for the evening meal. Dress consisted of tailcoat, satin breeches, silk stockings, and buckled shoes. Later there came more studying and evening prayers. Then lights out was the order at eleven o'clock.

Such was the vigorous routine during five days of the week, with a half holiday on Saturday, and an easy routine on Sunday, consisting chiefly of church services.

President Witherspoon regarded Henry Lee as his star pupil and took pains to feed him the Witherspoon doctrines of self-determination and independence. Though the president of the college put forth his views by way of logic and illustration, he did not openly go campaigning throughout the countryside. Nevertheless, he was elected to the Continental Congress and was the only clergyman and the only college president to be a signer of the Declaration of Independence.

He realized that the boys must have some form of recreation and of assembling themselves together, and he therefore encouraged the formation of clubs. Young Henry embraced this idea and soon was a member of a group which called themselves the American Whig Society. The name was significant because in England the Whigs were the Parliamentary group, as opposed to the Tories, and as a group had favored the independent ideas of the colonials. That party in England was not wholly consistent, due to the uncertain leadership of their senior representative, Lord Chatham (the elder William Pitt). Chatham said in Parliament at one time, *"I* rejoice that America has resisted"—in other words, resisted certain oppressions. But later he said, "I would never consent to independence, never, never, never." However, the word "Whig" was definitely a defiance of the Tory government, and Henry Lee in promoting the name was declaring himself. The society name became shortened to Whig, and it became clear that a competitive society would be desirable. Hence, Lee also had a part in the formation of Clio. Whig and Clio have continued as historic intellectual societies in Princeton over the generations. In pre-Revolutionary times they provided a forum for debate on the issues of the day.

The boys, however, did not confine themselves to literary pursuits. Fistfights were frequent, and there was some amount of carousing in the town. Many of the boys patronized brothels which had grown up in the community, but Lee refused to participate. Illicit sex did not interest him at that time or later. When he returned home from college, his father asked him if he would like to be introduced to a brothel, and Henry replied that he would not, that he had too much regard for the family name. It was not that he was undersexed; he ultimately married twice and fathered about a dozen children, including Robert E. Lee.

Lee's chief pleasure was in riding horseback. In this he was so proficient that he earned from his fellow students the nickname Light-Horse Harry. After his college days he was always known by that nickname, and the name Henry disappears from references to him.

Harry became one of the stalwart young men on whom Washington could rely; he stood by the commander throughout the war, but because Lee was a friend of the Washington family, the commander leaned backward to avoid granting him any special favors. Harry did not seek favors, but he worried lest he be completely cold-shouldered. In fact, when he was instructed to take a furlough at one point, even though he had not sought a vacation, he inquired of Alexander Hamilton, now Washington's administrative agent, as to whether this was a polite way of dismissing him from the army. Hamilton replied no—his mother and Martha Washington had concocted the idea as they felt that he needed a rest, and had prevailed upon the commander to agree to that.

When Harry first engaged in assistance for the Continental Army, he was an independent raider, and he captured many vital stores for the colonials. The British at first were lavishly supplied with wagonloads of ammunition, food, medicines, cattle, and even horses. They had no conception that they would need adequate defenders around their supply trains. In fact, usually the supply wagons marched behind the fighting force, which made it doubly easy for Light-Horse Harry and his informal troop to capture these supplies. The British general, Clinton, finally became so disturbed at these depredations that he exclaimed, "I expected the colonials to nip at our heels, but did not expect them to draw blood."

Though Harry was still a raider during the winter of Valley Forge, the supplies which he captured had a large part in enabling that poverty-stricken Army to survive. Periodically Lee's forces swooped down on the British cattle supply and drove away twenty or thirty head to the Valley Forge camp, where there was great rejoicing at the promise of steak dinners.

Lee also brought in medicines, ammunition, and clothing. On one occasion, he captured a truckload of wool cloth which had been dyed red; it could not be converted to blue, so it was cut up into blankets for the colonial troops.

Harry was aided by the fact that the British on one hand regarded the colonials as stupid, and on the other hand were obsessed by the idea of formalized order. An army had its supplies located in quartermaster wagons behind the main fighting forces and protected only by a small rear guard. That was the system, and that was the way they did it. As a result, they made an incredible amount of supplies available to the colonial forces.

As can be imagined, the entire economy of the colonies was in a state of confusion. The bulk of the Army supplies were hijacked by these raiders from British supply trains. There was little in the way of domestic manufacture because of shortage of labor, and deliveries to retail stores were erratic because of the uncertainties of transportation. Nevertheless, some shops were able to keep open by selling goods which were produced locally plus some that were obtained from British sources. The display of British goods was considered unpatriotic, and in the College of New Jersey the students were outraged at this lack of loyalty by local merchants. Hence, led by Lee, a mob of students swarmed down on Nassau Street and threatened each storekeeper that he would find himself no longer in business unless he confined himself to selling American goods.

The threat was obvious. The store could be wrecked or burned to the ground. All the merchants agreed to comply.

Looking back on the incident, Lee expressed regrets in his memoirs, saying that such conduct was against all concepts of law and order, that though he was only fifteen years of age he should have known better, that mob action was the opposite of an orderly society, and that he who had committed himself to law should not have participated in such an action.

Raiding enemy supply trains, however, he considered a legitimate act of war, not related to civilian life.

In the earlier stages of his military career, he operated virtually without portfolio. He did hold a captaincy in the forces of General Bland, but he was free to rove about as he might choose. At one point, Washington, sending the invitation through Alexander Hamilton, offered to take Lee on his headquarters staff. That was a high honor, and Lee felt some hesitancy in declining, lest he offend the commander-in-chief. However, he felt that he had no gift for administration and so passed the word back, hoping to be excused and to be permitted to continue with the work of military raids on the enemy, plus his services in spying and reporting to headquarters.

Lee had a gift for analyzing military situations. In college he had studied the campaigns of great generals in the past and could correlate this knowledge with the potentialities of what the British might do in the disposition of their forces. With the advantage of his swift horsemanship, he could ride into an area, take in at a glance location of the enemy, and ride off again, often before his presence was even known. Washington obviously found his reports useful and gave him permission to continue as an official spy, but warned him under no circumstances to be caught wearing civilian clothes. Under the customs of war, an enemy civilian found snooping around military operations could be hanged as a spy forthwith. Major André made that mistake and paid for it with his life. Lee obeyed those instructions unquestioningly, but he hoped for an assignment of more distinction.

That soon came to him. He was ordered to report to Gen. Nathanael Greene, in command of the Army of the South. The

British had assigned Lord Cornwallis, their most active general, to capture all the Southern strongholds and to strengthen the numerous forts already in the hands of the British. It was a grand design, because if the large area of the South could be subjugated, the war might be brought to a close in favor of Great Britain. The prospects of Cornwallis looked good, especially as the troops under Tarleton were already operating in the South and Tarleton was a gifted cavalry operator. Lee was to be his opposite number, a challenge which Light-Horse Harry welcomed.

Before taking on the assignment in the South, Harry had another project of a daring nature for which he needed the endorsement of General Washington. This project was the capture of Paulus Hook, on the surface an impossible scheme. Paulus Hook was a British fortress on a peninsula of the north Jersey coast; it commanded the approach to New York harbor and was an effective barrier to uniting the colonial forces to the north and south of that area. The fort was protected in front by the lower reaches of the Hudson River, in back by the Hackensack River and a creek which served the purpose of a moat. Warships were stationed on the main front of the fort, effectively protecting it from colonial naval attack. The only way to capture the garrison would be to get into the rear entrance by stealth with a force sufficient to overpower and capture the defenders. Such a project appeared to be so impossible that it had not even been considered by the chief strategists of the colonial forces.

Harry realized that the utmost secrecy would be important and that he must have full authority to direct the expedition. Hence, he put the matter before General Washington. It was part of the genius of Washington that he would listen to any proposition, and from any source, hoping that it might have merit. Lee was sure of his ground and had worked out the campaign in detail: where his forces would land, the time of night that they would start, the means for bridging the moat, the amount of time required to invest the fort and capture and remove the garrison—all this to be done before daylight.

Washington was impressed by the thoroughness with which the details had been worked out, but he was skeptical. Everything had to go right or the failure would be conspicuous and disastrous. A single defector could tip off the enemy and ruin the whole project.

Lee assured his commander that he personally knew every man who would be allowed on the expedition, that he had discussed the plan with his picked forces and had convinced everyone that the job could be done. Washington emphasized that while the glory and practical usefulness of success were great, failure by the same token would be intolerable. Lee kept returning to the argument with ardent persuasions. Washington at last gave his grudging consent. Hence, finally, at midnight, Lee alerted his little band for the attack. The crux of the matter was to assemble a bridge which could be thrown across the moat, permitting Lee's troops to enter the rear of the fort. The necessary bridge had been built and was thrown across the moat without arousing the sleeping garrison. At this point, a Major Clarke was able to see the probability of success and demanded of Lee to know the date of his commission. Clarke's point was that if Lee had a later commission than Clarke, Clarke was entitled to take over the command. Lee shrugged off the suggestion impatiently, saying that he had direct authority from General Washington, which was not transferrable.

Lee's troops swiftly and quietly entered the fortress, surprising the sleeping garrison. The fort had seemed so impregnable that the Britishers evidently had not given any thought to the possibility of attack. Most of the sleeping men were bundled out of the fort with little opposition, hardly aware of what was going on. All the captives were hurried down the lines to the American encampment and made prisoner without difficulty. Lee left a containing force within the fort, which was now in the possession of the colonials, and brought the remainder of his forces back to the mainland, all before daybreak. Then he sent a report of the good news to the commander-in-chief.

Lee naturally expected great commendation from all sides, but instead he found that he had committed the unpardonable sin of going over the heads of his Army superiors and carrying out an unorthodox project. The first complainer was Major Clarke, who felt that he had been robbed of a victory. He had approved the project, had been present while it was carried out, and as the ranking officer should have been allowed to command the enterprise. Equally enraged, if not more so, were two generals in the area who obviously outranked Light-Horse Harry and deplored any expedition's being carried out without their knowledge. The offense against military protocol was a sin that could not be redeemed by the victory of an unauthorized expedition. They demanded that Lee face a court-martial.

Washington did not intervene, as he knew that Lee was within his rights and that a court-martial would undoubtedly justify him. Harry was disappointed and infuriated. Instead of being publicly paraded as a national hero, he was to be forced to endure this court-martial in which he publicly would be attacked as guilty of something or other, and the public would wonder what it was all about. He was charged, of course, with insubordination, proceeding without orders from his superior officers, and general neglect of normal behavior.

Lee had but one defense. Namely, that he acted with the knowledge and permission of the commander-in-chief. That, of course, was conclusive, and the trial ended by clearing his name completely. Thenceforth he was the hero of Paulus Hook. Also his transfer to the staff of General Greene freed him from any reprisals by the officers to whom his conduct had been so offensive.

General Washington now came to the aid of Lee, granting him the honors that had been so long delayed. By the commander's recommendation Lee was promoted to the rank of lieutenant colonel. Various of his lieutenants were advanced to the rank of captain, the Continental Congress voted $15,000 to the noncommissioned officers and privates in such a manner as Washington would direct, and the latter agreed to accept the advice of Lee on that subject.

Moreover, Lee was voted the warm congratulations of Congress; a special Congressional Medal was struck and was awarded to him in a ceremony over which Washington presided. After all of that activity the question was how Lee should be occupied until the time for him to joint the staff of General Greene. Lee was allowed to outline his own plan of what would be an effective operating force. He proposed that he should be provided with his troop of cavalry supported by infantry troops which would also be under his direction. He was given the choice of cavalry units and of most of the infantry who had served with him at Paulus Hook. The total unit amounted to about five hundred men. It was organized within a month's time and became nicknamed Lee's Legion. Harry spent his time gathering supplies including provisions, blankets, saddles, and arms so that his "Legion" would take the field fully equipped. Furthermore, he was aware of the value of prestige for the new unit and provided each man with a uniform consisting of a plumed helmet, dark-green tunics, white breeches, and black boots. Harry rode in front of this group on his way to join Greene, and his cavalry and infantry learned how to work together by marching together. At length early in December, 1780, the "Legion" reached General Greene's headquarters on the banks of the Pee Dee River in South Carolina. He ordered his men to take a night's rest while he took a dinner conference with General Greene and General Francis Marion, who had been in charge of the Southern forces standing off the British invasion of the deep South. Marion and his followers were bearded and unkempt. They had been fighting in the woods and swamps for months. Marion was suspicious of this fancily dressed "Lee's Legion," which impressed him not at all, or rather adversely. He thought that they looked like young Britishers and wanted no truck with them. Greene, however, warned Lee to be tactful and to show great respect to Marion. Lee was sensible enough to take that advice, and soon he and Marion, known as the Old Swamp Fox, became fast friends.

CHAPTER XI

John Marshall

Pioneer Jurist

J OHN MARSHALL was one of the young men who were closest to George Washington and part of his unofficial family. He was born in 1755. Marshall won lasting fame as a chief justice who established the authority and most of the procedures of the Supreme Court, but his ideas were formulated in his early days. He served at Valley Forge and later said that at that time "I was confirmed in the habit of considering America my country and Congress my government."

Such a sentiment was evidence of an unusually mature mind, because the general attitude was to regard the various states as the real seat of authority.

Zeal for statism was one of the great handicaps to George Washington's military strategy, for several states would send militia to the Continental Army, give them orders, aı 1 recall them at will. Washington had the concept of the United States as a new nation, and he found this competitive authority on the part of the several states almost intolerable. He begged them to send their best men to Congress, so that that body might act with superior wisdom, but his requests were seldom granted.

In John Marshall, however, he had an ardent disciple. Marshall was only twelve when the so-called Townshend Acts of 1767 put a tax on tea and other products. These taxes were much resented by the colonies, who had no representation in the passing of these Parliamentary acts. Samuel Adams of Massachusetts sent a circular letter to the other colonies, asking them to protest these imposts. The British Government then sent an order to the various colonial governors to dissolve any assembly which approved the circular. Several had already done so, including Virginia, and their assembly was dissolved, but it met informally and drew up a nonimportation, nonconsumption agreement which was adopted by various other colonies. Most of the provisions of the Townshend Act were repealed, but the King insisted that the tax on tea be retained as a symbol of authority. Hence, during the early teens of John Marshall, the colonies were in a ferment over what they considered to be injustices.

Early biographies of John Marshall represented him as a poor backwoodsman of humble parentage who had risen to fame through his own efforts and abilities. That was the popular political style in the early days of the Republic, but in the case of Marshall it was only partly true. He had been born in a log cabin in the frontier hill country of Virginia. His father, Thomas Marshall, was a descendant of Welsh immigrants but was a man of distinction who had become known throughout the colonies. In his early manhood, Thomas had been an employee of George Washington, had fought in various skirmishes against the Indians, and had finally become a sheriff of his county, a profitable job. Later, Thomas sat in the House of Burgesses at Williamsburg. While his son John was still a boy, the family moved from the country to a village not far away, and they subsequently moved to a home near Goose Creek, which was within a few miles of the present Leesburg. Another feature of John's ancestry was that his mother had been a Randolph, of the famous Virginia family. Through this connection he was related to Thomas Jefferson and a host of other famous cousins. Hence this young man of supposedly humble stock actually had superior connections.

His education was informal. He attended the College of William and Mary for a few weeks at one time in his life, but he was mostly educated by tutors. That was the usual procedure in the case of families who lived in rural regions. John's father, saw to it that the boy had first-class tutors. These were clergymen who instructed the boy in literature, Latin, and Greek In his early teens, John was reading Horace, Livy, and the great classics. His favorite English author was Pope, and he wrote commentaries on that author's "Essay on Man."

Thomas Marshall was a brainy character who kept up with current thought. When the first American edition of Blackstone's *Commentaries* was published, the elder Marshall was one of the first subscribers.

The young man's upbringing was uneventful until his father heard news of the Battle of Lexington. He called John into the living room and, taking down from the wall his rifle and the hunting knife, said to his son, "This means war."

Not many Southerners were so sure of that fact at the time, for Lexington had been a little action near far away Boston. But Thomas Marshall was sure that the matter would not end there. Hence, he drilled the boy in the manual of arms and soon arranged that the two of them would become officers in a militia company. That company in turn was merged with the Continental Army under George Washington and soon was engaged in a major battle at Brandywine, near Philadelphia.

In this affair, the colonials were outnumbered by the Redcoats under Howe. The Redcoats had an ample supply of firearms and had the advantage of training as regulars. The colonials were

98

hardly more than a mob. Some had seen service in wars against the Indians, but many had never been in battle before and were easily frightened. John, on this occasion, struck up a friendship with Lafayette, who was wounded in battle; young Marshall endured a similar fate when he suffered a bullet in the leg. Both he and Lafayette escaped to the hospital in Bethlehem, Pennsylvania, which the Moravians maintained for the care of wounded soldiers.

The question has been raised why Howe didn't pursue his advantage and wipe out the Continental Army. Some give him credit for a friendly feeling toward the colonial cause and a hope that peace by negotiation would be obtained. Others have speculated that he and fellow officers took such a beating at Bunker Hill when they attacked the colonial forces that Howe had no zeal for combat with the colonists again. Both explanations could be true. The fact is that Howe never did seek a major encounter with Washington's army, and he enjoyed a comfortable, almost luxurious, sojourn in Philadelphia until he resigned his command, believing that the War Office had lost confidence in him.

Contemporary memoirs say that the Philadelphia period was a constant succession of dinner parties, balls, and theatrical entertainments. Major André, who was later caught as a spy in the attempted betrayal of West Point, was a leading spirit in this Philadelphia social season. The neighboring farmers kept the British supplied with ample quantities of meat, fowl, and vegetables, while the colonial troops had difficulty getting enough food for subsistence.

Meanwhile, Lafayette and John Marshall, recuperating at the hands of the Moravians, found their accommodations difficult. The hospital quarters were vastly overcrowded. There were normal accommodations for possibly two hundred patients, whereas about one thousand had swarmed into this little community, seeking help.

In due course, Lafayette and Marshall recovered and joined Washington's forces at Valley Forge. As history knows, it was a hideous winter. The soldiers lacked adequate clothing, blankets, and heat. They were quartered in a number of huts and frequently stayed awake most of the night in order to keep the fires going.

In this gloomy situation, Marshall was an aid to morale, for he never seemed to be downcast and he enjoyed unusual health. His rural upbringing had given him a stalwart physique, and he was the best athlete in the camp. He had a practice of balancing a pole on the heads of two of his comrades, then vaulting over it. He was also the swiftest runner. His mother had sent him a pair of socks which she had knitted; she had made the heels of white wool. In the foot races which Marshall organized, he, like the others, ran without shoes, as shoes were virtually unobtainable. Hence, as he dashed along, the white heels of his socks were conspicuous and won him the nickname Silver Heels.

The situation of the troops was not as bad as sometimes reported because, as we know from a prior chapter, Light-Horse Harry Lee had developed great skill in seizing British supply wagons and even in driving off herds of cattle to the American camp. This type of action appealed to Marshall, and he arranged to be part of Lee's expeditions, an arrangement which lasted through many months and resulted in a lifelong friendship between the two men.

Marshall's temperament was happy-go-lucky, cheerful, and fair-minded. Men who had disputes would come to him to have their differences settled and would abide by his decisions. When disputes got tense, he would think up some practical joke, some prank, that would cause laughter and remove the hard feelings.

Marshall was also a great comfort to Washington in more serious situations. He got wind of the fact that General Gates was leading a movement to have himself made commander-in-chief instead of Washington. Gates maintained that he had won the

100

Battle of Saratoga, where Burgoyne had been defeated. It is true that he was in command on that occasion, though other officers had played a major part in the achievement. At any rate, Gates claimed that he had won a great victory, whereas Washington had endured a series of humiliating defeats. Gates had persuaded others of the rightness of his cause. One of his colleagues was named Conway, and this move to unseat Washintgon was known as the Conway Cabal.

By learning of the plot in advance through Marshall, Washington was able to thwart it. Furthermore, his position was strengthened by his success at the Battle of Trenton, where during the Christmas holiday he bagged several hundred Hessians who did not expect such an attack.

The capture of Burgoyne's army, which was fully exploited by the diplomacy of Benjamin Franklin in Paris, led to the decision of France to come to the aid of the Americans, and the French king announced that decision on May 6, 1778. That was an enormous boost for the Continental Army. France promised money, military supplies, and the aid of the French fleet. In fact, victory was virtually in sight, even though it was three years more before the British admitted defeat.

One of the major battles in which Marshall was to take part was fought at Monmouth, New Jersey. Washington's army was driving the British from the field, when to his great surprise and rage one of the generals, Charles Lee (no relative of the American Lees), attempted to lead his men in retreat. Washington, enraged, bawled the man out in front of the General Staff. Marshall, who always believed in fair play, thought that Washingon had been unduly rough, but in this case Marshall was not aware of all the circumstances.

Lee had been a soldier of fortune who had fought with the British in earlier years and then subsequently had embraced the

101

colonial cause. He had been disappointed at his lack of recognition by Washington. Whether his attempted retreat was simple coward-ice or whether it was intended to ingratiate him with the British is not known. But his former British colleagues had a dim opinion of him. Lord Dartmouth wrote to Lord Amherst: "Having hap-pened to hear a little of General Lee before he left England, I have always considered him as a mad man. However, it is very certain that mad men are sometimes capable of giving a great deal of trouble to those who are more in their senses than them-selves."

Lee had not only attempted to retreat but had ignored Wash-ington's command to advance. His defection had slowed the pace of the American attack, which at first was driving the British Army into a rout, but they now escaped before the American forces could overtake them. Lee was brought before a court-martial, which led to his suspension. Sir Joseph Yorke, the British ambassa-dor to Holland, heard of it. Knowing that Amherst had had trouble with Lee in earlier years, he wrote to Amherst: "What has diverted me highly has been to see that fellow Lee suspended for mis-behavior and cowardice by those American heroes. They have paid old scores for all of us with that intractable fellow who was to drive us out of America. I could not help laughing at this for an hour together."

This battle was almost the last in John Marshall's military ex-perience, though he participated in one more dramatic event, an affair which has been mentioned previously. He was present at the American capture of the fort at Paulus Hook. He was with Light-Horse Harry Lee on that famous midnight raid. He was present when the American troops captured the bewildered de-fenders and led them down the road to the American headquarters, where they were made prisoners of war. It was a heartwarming climax to his military career.

His term of enlistment was up, and he was not assigned to any further engagement by the Continental Army. He had put in several useful years and was ready to pursue his study of law. This he accomplished shortly. He married and established a law practice in Richmond, Virginia. From then on, he had increasing success, both in legal triumphs and in public service to America. Those events, however, came after his youth and are not a part of our story here.

CHAPTER XII

James Monroe

Independent Fighter

J AMES MONROE, born in 1758, a future President of the United
States, was one of the youngest of the Revolutionary warriors,
and an independent among the famous Virginia fighters.

Monroe, in short, was not one of the famous coterie on Washington's personal staff who upheld the commander through his darkest
hours. Monroe did not belong to that upper-crust society, possibly
did not know them socially. His parents were of good Virginia
stock, what today might be described as upper middle class.

The parents were ambitious for James, sent him to a private
school, and entered him at the College of William and Mary at the
age of sixteen.

The war broke out two years later, and Monroe promptly enlisted
as a lieutenant in a Virginia regiment. He sought action and was
present at the battles of Harlem, White Plains, and Trenton. In
the last engagement he was wounded in the shoulder. He also
faced fire at Brandywine, Germantown, and Monmouth.

His valor was noticed by Washington, but he attracted the particular attention of General Stirling,* who made Monroe his aide with the rank of major. Stirling was one of Washington's principal generals and loyal to him in several crises. Stirling, however, had his own staff and did most of his own recruiting. Monroe accordingly was in that branch of the service, and when he sought to return to a Virginia regiment in 1780 there was no suitable place available. His uncle advised him that he had done sufficient fighting for any hero and should undertake the civilian study of law. Hence he became a pupil in the office of Thomas Jefferson, who was then governor of Virginia. That move proved to be an auspicious start for Monroe's future career.

---

* The General is frequently referred to as the Earl of Stirling or Lord Stirling, titles which he claimed to merit. He was, in fact, a blood relative of the British peers of that name, but his family had taken part in the Stuart uprising and had fled to America after the defeat at Culloden. All who had taken part in the Stuart cause were stripped of their British honors. His civilian name was William Alexander, but he did not use it.

CHAPTER XIII

Campus Revolutionaries

One of the outstanding phenomena of the American Revolution is that nearly all of the undergraduates of the existing universities departed en masse to serve the cause. Most of them went into active military service and at the very least were sympathizers.

There were nine universities in existence in the colonies prior to the Declaration of Independence.* These will be listed shortly, and a separate report on the participation of each campus is appended to this chapter. It will be noted that both the administration and the faculty of each institution were pro-Revolution. In two cases the presiding head had remained loyal to the home government. The head of King's College (Columbia), Myles Cooper, fearing the wrath of the students who had stormed up in front of his house, escaped out of the back door and fled to the home of a

---

* This chapter has several sections dealing with the colleges in revolutionary days. The various sections are referred to under their colonial names, which in some instances were different from names today. The sections, however, are listed alphabetically according to their current names: Brown, Columbia, Dartmouth, Harvard, Pennsylvania, Princeton, Rutgers, William and Mary, Yale.

106

friend who lived near the harbor. The incident is detailed in the section on Columbia. The Provost of Pennsylvania, a Loyalist, fled to escape the wrath of the Patriots.

Youth is typically rebellious and critical of the preceding generation, but there was more than that factor in this widespread adherence of the campus to the colonial principles. The other factor was the method of teaching which had prevailed in nearly all the universities with the exception of William and Mary.

In general the curriculum followed the pattern advocated by the Jesuits which was prevalent in France. Instead of teaching separate subjects as was usual in the British universities, the emphasis was on moral laws and classroom discussions. The subject matter taught was similar in each of the colleges. The method was termed *scholasticism*. It reverted back to the Middle Ages and dealt primarily with ethics and philosophy. Even in anti-Catholic New England the method was followed without reference to the source.

Essentially, the student was educated by a continuous disputation and exploration of ideas, which he could defend or attack as he chose. At graduation time, the seniors distributed printed broadsides of the theses to be advanced, and members of the audience were given copies so that they would be in a position to ponder and enter into the debates if they wished. The nature of these theses will give an idea of how the thinking of the students would inevitably be slanted. The theses were not limited to politics, as such. They also covered rhetoric, grammer, logic, physics, ethics, and jurisprudence. In the theses of the University of Pennsylvania, 1763, the declarations on politics read as follows:

1. That civil power is alone just which makes for the common benefit.
2. The rights of the people are as divine as those of their rulers.

107

3. Lawmakers and landowners should always follow a true course and never selfishly, by the same token, fail to seek out the proof thereof.
4. Those who throw down their arms and entrust themselves to the faith of their rulers should be received.
5. It is the duty of the advocate or patron always in legal trials to follow the truth and never to defend falsehood knowingly even though it should seem very like the truth.
6. For the cherishing of every virtue in a city the most potent influence is the example set by the rulers.
7. To have snatched anyone from death or from any other evil does not confer the right of reducing him into slavery.

Item number 2 is clearly indicative of the independent attitude of the public: "The rights of the people are as divine as those of their rulers." That certainly forecast a doubt about the intrinsic authority of the Crown. Nor was that an isolated accidental expression. In another thesis appears the expression: "The right authority among men does not arrive from any superior dignity of nature."

Still another thesis said: "Where right ends, there injury begins, and the right of existence asserts itself."

This system of education obviously was inimical to the unquestioning acceptance of authority, and it encouraged self-determination.

There was one specific requirement—to take Latin and usually enough Greek to enable the student to read the New Testament. Latin, in fact, was the universal language of scholars, and it was a considerable loss to scholarship when that ceased to be the case. In later years there were movements to create an international language, such as Esperanto, but that need had already been met by Latin, which had been largely abandoned except by lawyers and the Roman Catholic Church. It is strange that there was no general protest against the decline in the ability to read and speak Latin. Possibly both the church and the law enjoyed having their little pocket of knowledge which was not understood by the commoners.

Though instruction at the College of William and Mary was similar to that in the English universities, the feeling of independence was strong there also. The populace from whom the students were drawn consisted of persons who had established their own careers independently of any support from the home government. Their occupations were largely agricultural, ranging from the vast plantations to little farms. The wealthy plantation owners were virtually the ruling authority in their own domains and were resentful of interference from across the Atlantic.

The late Christian Gauss, former dean of students at Princeton, has said that any institution must have the backing of the church and the universities if it is to prevail. In colonial times the church and the academy were interrelated. The cause of education was underwritten by the church. The purpose of some universities, as specifically stated, was to train young men for the Christian ministry and/or teaching. In many a community the minister and the schoolteacher were the two learned men. Sometimes one man performed both services. Medicine and law were specialized functions, and only the larger communities had the fully rounded

The church was the initial supporter of all the early universities, either financially or at least through its public approval. Thus we find that three of the nine pre-Revolutionary colleges were insti-

services of all the professions.

tuted under Congregational auspices, three Episcopal, and one each Presbyterian, Baptist, and Dutch Reformed.

The status of the nine colonial colleges is given in the following list showing the date of founding of each, dates of changes in name, and the determination of church support.

109

Colleges in Existence Before the American Revolution

HARVARD COLLEGE: Congregational
Cambridge, Massachusetts
October 28, 1636, College
1780, University

COLLEGE OF WILLIAM AND MARY: Episcopal
Williamsburg, Virginia
February 8, 1693, College
1779, University

YALE COLLEGE: Congregational
New Haven, Connecticut
October 16, 1701, College
1887, University

COLLEGE OF NEW JERSEY (PRINCETON): Presbyterian
Princeton, New Jersey
October 22, 1746, College
1896, Princeton University

KING'S COLLEGE (COLUMBIA): Episcopal
New York, New York
October 31, 1754
1784, Columbia College
1896, Columbia University

COLLEGE OF PHILADELPHIA (PENNSYLVANIA): Episcopal
Philadelphia, Pennsylvania
June 16, 1755, College
1791, University of Pennsylvania

RHODE ISLAND COLLEGE (BROWN): Baptist
Providence, Rhode Island
October 24, 1764
1804, Brown University

QUEEN'S COLLEGE (RUTGERS): Dutch Reformed
New Brunswick, New Jersey
November 10, 1766
1825, Rutgers College
1924, Rutgers University

DARTMOUTH COLLEGE: Congregational
Hanover, New Hampshire
December 12, 1769

The rest of this chapter will present a report on each of these American colleges that were in existence before the Revolution, showing what part each had in the conflict in respect both to influence and to actual participation. The reports are in alphabetical order of the names by which they are known today. For example, the date of the founding of any particular college did not necessarily have any relevance to the depth of its patriotic zeal; both Rhode Island College and Yale were conspicuous in their ardor for independence though the time of their founding was many years apart.

The reports vary in length not because of relative importance but because of the simplicity or complexity of each college's involvement. For example, Yale was inescapably involved in the Revolution both by its geographic location and through the dramatic heroism of its alumnus, Nathan Hale, and yet its story is simple and quickly told. On the other hand, the University of Pennsylvania had a complicated structure in its early days. It

111

was founded by Benjamin Franklin, for a time had a Tory president, but ultimately became committed to the American cause. A recital of its situation requires more detail than a simple story such as that of Yale, or Dartmouth.

Brown (Rhode Island College)

Rhode Island College was perhaps the most belligerent of the pre-Revolutionary colleges. A tablet in University Hall states that faculty, students, and graduates, almost to a man, were engaged in service to their country in the Revolutionary War.

Chartered in 1764, Brown was known initially as the Rhode Island College at Warren, but in its early days it received substantial gifts from the Brown family and through the years it has had continuing contributions from that source.

The first president of Rhode Island College was the Rev. Dr. James Manning, a graduate of the College of New Jersey. The college was sponsored by the Baptist denomination. Eight of the twelve fellows and twenty-two of the thirty-six trustees were required by the charter to be of the Baptist denomination. However, four of the board were members of the Congregational Church, five were Episcopalians, and five were Quakers. A gift of $5,000 from the Brown family in 1804, and subsequent gifts amounting to $160,000 led to the ultimate naming of the college.

Various charter provisions indicated the temper of the institution. One was that there should never be permitted "any religious tests, but on the contrary all the members hereof shall forever enjoy full, absolute and uninterrupted liberty of conscience." Again the charter provided that "the sectarian differences of opinion shall not make any part of the public and classical instruction." A third proviso was that "the public teaching shall in general respect the sciences."

112

That general platform declaimed against various prejudices of the day. It refused to admit the authority of any one creed, and it recognized the validity of scientific teaching, which was a matter of great controversy at that time.

These strong declarations of an open mind as opposed to the various types of intolerance of that day naturally opened the way to unfettered discussion of the principles that led to the Revolution.

Rhode Island, like several other colonial colleges, had the system of teaching by disputations. It also presented printed theses and arguments for discussion at commencement times. One of the basic theses was that "all power of making laws and inflicting penalties is derived from the people." By implication that was a denial of the supreme authority of the Crown. Another thesis was that for a legislature to impose taxes on people who are not represented is not just. That was a preliminary to the affirmation of the Revolution that there should be no taxation without representation.

Initially the propositions discussed were inclined to discourage revolutionary activity as such; but by 1774 the general tenor had changed, even before Lexington, and at that time there were several inflammatory theses including these:

Anyone who takes away liberty from another is unworthy to enjoy his own liberty.

A defensive war is licit.

Unjust laws often impel men to make revolution.

Dozens of other examples might be given, for year after year the tenor of the theses was liberty of conscience and liberty of opinion.

When the war finally came the college was closed for about six years, for it had neither students nor faculty and was under

113

frequent attack from the enemy. Fully as much as and possibly more than any other college, it gave its entire physical and moral strength to the cause of independence.

Columbia (King's College)

Columbia University, known in colonial days as King's College, might have been expected to be a particular pet of the Crown, and loyal to the Tory government, to judge by its name. That, however, would not be a correct impression.

One of the leading societies at the university has been known as King's Crown, and its members use a pin in the shape of a crown as their symbol. That is merely poetic license, however, as King's College was governed not by the Crown but by a board of governors (trustees), who administered the college financially and academically and who elected its presidents.

King's College had been created by royal charter in 1754, but the driving force behind the establishment of the university was local. The financial support was provided by the local citizens. Great Britain's interest expressed itself through the Church of England rather than through the Government.

The citizens who originally sought to establish the college requested Rev. Dr. Samuel Johnson to become its first president. Johnson had become famous throughout the colonies because of his participation in religious and philosophical controversy. He originally had been a Congregationalist, but ultimately found "the Congregational way" unsatisfactory. During a trip abroad, he was ordained in the Church of England, and on his return to America he became the first Episcopal divine in Connecticut. Hence the influence of that church was predominant from the early days of the college, and continued to be so.

When Johnson needed an assistant, the Archbishop of Canterbury recommended Dr. Myles Cooper, who was accepted by the trustees. Johnson served until 1763, when he resigned because of ill health and was succeeded by Cooper. During Cooper's administration, the struggle between the colonists and Great Britain became increasingly intense. One of the leading agitators on the colonial side was the nineteen-year-old Alexander Hamilton, a student at King's College, whose oratory and logic dominated undergraduate opinion in favor of colonial revolt. In May, 1775, a mob of students gathered at the president's house, possibly with the intent to lynch him. At any rate, Cooper was taking no chances. Clad only in his nightshirt, he fled out the back door of his house, making his way to the river. Hamilton, though an ardent colonial, held the student mob in check, giving Cooper adequate time to escape. Hamilton had sense enough to know that the lynching of a college president would not help the colonial cause in the eyes of the world. Cooper was able to board a ship for England, and he never returned to this country.

Among other King's College graduates who became famous were John Jay, Gouverneur Morris, Philip Van Cortlandt, Robert R. Livingston, and Henry Rutgers.

The independence of the United States, and the Revolutionary War period, led to the virtual disbanding of the college for several years. In April, 1776, the Committee of Safety of the Continental Congress demanded that the governors of King's College prepare their buildings to receive troops. The students were dispersed, and most of the facilities were converted to a military hospital. By 1777, there were only two students registered, and for eight years the college was out of operation. It continued to be in existence as a legal entity and was reorganized in the acts of the New York State legislature in 1784. The authority formerly vested in the Board of Governors of King's College was transferred to the Regents of the State of New York, under the name of Columbia

College. In 1787, the authority was transferred again to the Board of Trustees of Columbia, under whose successors the university is still operating.

Dartmouth

Dartmouth College, founded in 1769, was a pro-colonial institution from the beginning. The bulk of its original financial support came from England, but from Britishers who were sympathetic to colonial rights, notably Lord Dartmouth.

Its chief founder was Eleazer Wheelock, a Congregational minister from Connecticut who had created an academy for the education and Christianizing of the Indians. He had a board of trustees who were citizens of Connecticut, but their funds were not adequate to transform the academy into a college. Wheelock accordingly turned to England to raise funds. His academy had a good reputation among religious dissenters. It also had met with considerable criticism. The chief critic was Sir William Johnson, the government officer in charge of Indian affairs. Johnson was a champion of the Five Nations Indian Tribe in New York State, a group which had developed a notable civilization of their own, and Johnson was their powerful patron. He objected to missionaries' trying to convert the Indians who had a different way of life and belief. He alleged that the Indian youths who attended the Wheelock Academy became lazy and arrogant, and he attempted to discourage British citizens from contributing to this project for a college. However, two proponents of the college campaigned for many months in Britain, speaking before churches and societies, taking up collections for their purpose. They met with considerable success.

Certain clergy of the Church of England resented this activity on the part of the dissenters and raised the question how anyone

116

knew whether the money would go for the stated purpose or whether it would merely be pocketed by these traveling solicitors. Wheelock agreed that the money should be put into a trust fund separate from the trust he had established in Connecticut. The question then was who should be head of the English trust. It was important to have a man who would inspire confidence. The choice settled upon the Earl of Dartmouth, known to be sympathetic to the colonies, and he agreed to be president of the trust.

Wheelock's chief trouble seemed to be over. There was still a major decision ahead: where to locate the college, which so far existed only as an idea. There seemed to be no satisfactory available site in Connecticut. Various small parcels of land were offered, but nothing the size suitable for a campus. Then the small village of Hanover in northern New Hampshire offered a block of 3,000 acres to induce the founding of the college there. They felt that it would serve to pacify the Indians in the area, and Indians were always a potential threat to colonial settlements.

The question now arose as to what should be the name of the college. Wentworth, the Crown governor of New Hampshire, was an ambitious man, and Wheelock thought to flatter him by suggesting that perhaps the college might best be named for him. Alternatively Wheelock suggested the name of Dartmouth. This was a smooth bit of maneuvering on Wheelock's part. Wentworth was complimented at the suggestion of the college's being named for him, but he felt that the suggestion of his own name in competition with the Earl of Dartmouth would be impolitic. Hence the question of the name was settled.

Then came the question of what would be the policy of the college. From the beginning it sponsored the rights of the colonials. Lord Dartmouth was an early advocate of self-government for the various provinces. Three years after the founding of the college in

1772, he became secretary of state for the Colonies. It may be recalled from another chapter that Dartmouth proposed to the King and Cabinet a redress of colonial grievances and the adoption of a set of policies that would satisfy the economic development of the colonies under a system of self-government. In fact what Dartmouth proposed was well ahead of his time. Various colonies would under his plan enjoy what today would be regarded as dominion status.

The King and Cabinet wholly rejected Lord Dartmouth's plan, looked upon his attitude as subversive, and removed him to an unimportant post in the government. He was succeeded by Lord George Germain, who was committed to a "firm policy." Dartmouth persisted in his personal views and looked upon this college in America as an outpost of liberty. When war broke out in 1775 and the Howe brothers were appointed to suppress the rebellion, Dartmouth requested that "the safety of the college might be recommended to both General Sir William Howe and his brother, the admiral."

Tradition says that there never was a Tory on the campus at Hanover, and before the war was over it is said that the entire student body had enlisted in the colonial cause. While Dartmouth College has been relatively ignored in the history of the Revolution, its strategic importance was great. Its location at Hanover was close to Canada. The governor of New Hampshire, residing in the eastern part of the state, was a Crown appointee and sympathetic to the home government. If Dartmouth College had been on the Tory side it could have been a serious threat to northern New England. In fact, it was an important protection against any danger from the north.

Its motto was a dramatic statement of its purpose: *vox clamantis in deserto*—"the voice of one crying in the wilderness."

Harvard

The rebellious temper of the Boston area, agitated by the various punitive measures against that city instigated by the Crown, was naturally reflected in the opinions of the Harvard students. Prior to the war, there were constant debates and oratory championing the American cause.

However, there was some Loyalist sentiment extant, and a few of the students were Tories. Loyalists among the students, to show their sentiments, drank tea.

Though Governor Hutchinson of Massachusetts favored the British position, he was an alumnus of the college and highly popular. The students gave a banquet in his honor, but this was offset by a similar dinner held in honor of John Hancock. Hancock was treasurer of the college and had been a notable Revolutionist since his early days.

The rebellious sentiments of the Harvard students were not particularly significant because they could hardly be otherwise considering the independent sentiment of eastern Massachusetts (the western part of the state was mostly rural and relatively inconspicuous from a political standpoint).

The Battle of Lexington on April 19, 1775, created a crisis in college affairs. The students were told to go home, and the buildings were taken over by the Crown.

The college moved to Concord temporarily. On April 3, 1776, the corporation and overseers, who had continued the nominal operation of Harvard, voted the degree of LL.D. to George Washington, the first person to receive that honor from the college. Washington had been appointed commander-in-chief of the Continental Army and at first had his headquarters in Cambridge, where he was laying siege to the British Army in Boston, forcing its utlimate evacuation. Hence, in June, 1776, the students reassembled in

119

Cambridge. The Declaration of Independence was imminent, and the students became inevitably committed to the cause.

Thus Harvard, more than any other colonial college, was wholly involved in the War for Independence because of its geographic location.

Harvard, of course, can boast of a most notable roster of Patriot alumni, such as Samuel Adams, John Adams, John Hancock, James Otis, Robert Treat Paine, Elbridge Gerry, and William Ellery.

Pennsylvania (College of Philadelphia)

Pennsylvania, and Philadelphia especially, have been regarded sometimes as having been hotbeds of Tory sympathy, but in fact their leaders in the main were strong supporters of the Revolution and had been preaching republican sentiments as early as 1740.

Benjamin Franklin, the instigator of what became the University of Pennsylvania, had conceived the need for an educational body as early as 1740 and had drawn up an actual plan by 1743. The plan developed into a three-division school: the charity school, the academy, and the college department.

Franklin, as everyone knows, was never a Tory and was one of the earliest advocates of colonial independence. He was a singular character to be a leader in Philadelphia society. He had come to the city from Boston, had married a plain but devoted woman, and had made a reputation as an editor and writer. Certainly he had no social status in the generally accepted sense of the term, and yet he won the support of leading men in Philadelphia.

The trustees of the foundation for the tripartite school included the names of Logan, Lawrence, Willing, Bond, Taylor, Hopkins, Peters, Shippen, Cadwalader, and Biddle. Most of that roster continue to be leading Philadelphia families today.

The governmental form of the province did not call for direct loyalty to the King, but rather to the proprietor, William Penn. He was the landlord of that area, and loyalty belonged to him in the first instance.

T. H. Montgomery, in his *History of the University of Pennsylvania,* states, "The college and the Academy turned into the arena of the Revolution more men in proportion to the graduates than any other college institution." This statement doubtless would be challenged by other pre-Revolutionary colleges, but it shows the sentiment of the Pennsylvanians.

The attitude of the undergraduates is indicated by the number who took part ultimately in the new government. Among the most famous was Francis Hopkinson, who became a signer of the Declaration. In the class of 1759 was William Paca, one of the signers, and Philemon Dickinson, a leading Patriot.

In the class of 1760 was Thomas Lipton, later a general in the Revolution; the Cadwalader brothers, who became prominent Patriots; and Whitmel Hill, active in the Revolution.

In the class of 1761 were other Patriot leaders, including Richard Peters, Tench Tilghman, and John Neilson.

In the 1762 graduating class was Samuel Jones, who was active in the founding of Rhode Island College (Brown).

It is significant of Washington's policy that he chose Tench Tilghman as his military secretary throughout the whole war. Tilghman was born in 1744 and was only seventeen when he was graduated from college, and his appointment on Washington's staff was typical of the fact that the general liked to be surrounded by young men.

Indeed, it may be reemphasized that younger men were the activists that could be depended upon, whereas the difficulties encountered by Washington, John Paul Jones, and other fighting men were created by the doubts, uncertainties, and meddling of the older, more conservative members of the Continental Congress.

The College of Philadelphia was general in the composition of its students, unlike the tradition in New England. The purpose here evidently was not solely to train students for the Christian ministry. Among the group of graduates of the Philadelphia college in early years, thirty-four became clergymen, sixteen physicians, and forty lawyers.

One may inquire why Philadelphia had the reputation of being a Loyalist center in spite of these indications to the contrary. The answer is that the city was headquarters for the British Army and Navy, with General Howe commanding the Army, and his brother Admiral Howe in charge of the Navy. The Howe brothers were known to be Whig sympathizers and were suspected of not desiring to defeat the colonies. They apparently hoped that some method of conciliation might be evolved. Consequently, the Howes did not impose their forces on Philadelphia as if it were a conquered city but rather made it a place of entertainment. There were many balls, banquets, and other social events at which leading colonial families were welcome. There was no attempt to make prisoners of the Patriot leaders, though indeed we find Patriot fathers warning their daughters not to get too involved with the Redcoat officers.

Another influence which cast a Tory suspicion was that Provost William Smith, who headed the College of Pennsylvania, was an avowed Loyalist. He had come from Scotland originally and was an ordained priest in the Church of England. At times during his administration he asserted the authority of the Crown, and at other times he preached on the rights of man.

However, there was a change of British military administration within a very short time. The Howe brothers were called home, and Sir Henry Clinton was appointed in their stead. Clinton changed his headquarters from Philadelphia to New York. The Continental Congress then visited the College of Philadelphia in a body, with Washington at its head, signaling the approval of the

Patriots in the institution. Provost Smith did not contend with the new regime, and the patriotism of the college was no longer suspect. Smith was forced to leave, and he fled into Maryland. In spite of his loyalty to the Crown, he clearly had no intention of returning to England. As soon as he arrived in Maryland, he set about establishing the Protestant Episcopal Church in America, which followed the doctrines of the Church of England. He was eager to be named bishop of the initial diocese, but unfortunately he had become a habitual drunkard. Dr. Benjamin Rush, who attended him and admired his mind and character in sober moments, nevertheless testified that Smith was almost constantly under the influence.

The spirit of the College of Philadelphia, despite the reservations of its original provost, appeared evident in the commencement exercises in 1775, when the son of the provost gave a commencement oration entitled "The Fall of Empire." In this he said:

> Liberty is our idol!—She is the parent of virtue, the guardian of innocence and the terror of vice. Equal laws, security of property, true religion, wisdom, magnanimity, arts and sciences, are her lovely offspring. She has turned deserts into fruitful fields and villages into populous cities. Without enjoying the blessings which she bestows, the solitary state of nature is preferable to society; and the skins of wild beasts a more honorable covering than all the silken vestments slavery can bestow.

Princeton (College of New Jersey)

Princeton University, its alumni, and the community have had a continuing historic role in the life of the nation. As we are dealing here with reports of the colonial influence of the colleges, we shall confine ourselves chiefly to that limited period.

The most influential person in bringing the college into support of the Revolution was Richard Stockton, who was a native of Princeton and was graduated in the class of 1748.

Stockton was the son of a landed family that had settled in Princeton some years before his birth. He had inherited several thousand acres, which included the property now known as Morven. There he bred horses and cattle, and for the manor house he collected art treasures and established a notable library. Morven ultimately was given to the state for use as the official residence of the governor.

Stockton had studied law following graduation, and he ultimately achieved a profitable practice, but much of his energy was devoted to the development of the college. He early became a trustee. He soon became a major influence in its policies and in the attitude of the Province of New Jersey.

Initially, Stockton was a moderate who desired to maintain good relations with Parliament and the Crown. He submitted two proposals to Great Britain which would have been acceptable to the colonies. One was that several seats in the British Parliament be allocated to the Americans. This was disdainfully rejected. The other proposal was the establishment of a self-governing American parliament, which would acknowledge loyalty to the King though not accepting any royal authority. This proposal likewise was rejected.

The students, of course, were aware of these goings-on and discused the issues in their debating societies.

It was evident that the British authorities had no conception of the colonial situation. Those Englishmen who had settled in America had strong convictions about the "liberty of the subject." Their protests and petitions were not the work of a rabble, but their leaders included the most substantial men in the New World.

When Princeton started looking for a new president, the trustees decided to issue a call to Rev. John Witherspoon of Glasgow.

That choice was significant, as Witherspoon had a reputation as a firebrand, a leader of a movement known as the Popular party. He advocated self-rule for the Presbyterian churches, with the right to decide on whom they wished to call as their pastors. Witherspoon had achieved prestige in his own country and abroad. He had been invited to accept pastorates both in Dublin and in Rotterdam but had declined. There was no assurance that Witherspoon would accept a call to Princeton, and hence Stockton, who happened to be abroad, was delegated to deliver the invitation personally. He did so but found his mission to be not an easy one. Witherspoon initially was intrigued by the idea, but his wife was opposed to leaving her Scottish home to settle in a strange land across the seas. Stockton finally prevailed, and Witherspoon arrived in America in 1768 to assume the presidency of the College of New Jersey.

Witherspoon's eminence as an American patriot is well known. He championed the cause of the colonies eloquently and became the only clergyman to sign the Declaration of Independence.

His influence among the students was notable. The majority were ardently pro-colonial, and the Tories among the undergraduates led a hard time. Those who had Tory parents were ducked under the water pump and otherwise mistreated. Witherspoon kept fanning the flames. He encouraged the students to discuss the issues of the day in the light of the rights of man. He became a leader in the community and a member of the Continental Congress.

The village of Princeton, compared to the other colonial colleges, was in an abnormally hazardous situation. It was inland and surrounded by land. From Boston the colonials could drive the enemy into the sea and could retreat into the hinterland for hundreds of miles. The men of Yale could retire along the many roads leading into various sections of Connecticut. The Philadelphia

Patriots could move into the back areas of Pennsylvania; but Princeton was a sitting duck. It sat on the one main highway of the area, and there was no lush back country to give it support.

The village and the college, however, had the advantage of a central location, and Nassau Hall, which housed the college, was the biggest building in the colonies. The town taverns were focal points for stagecoach travel. Sometimes as many as twenty coaches departed in one day. There were one hundred horses in the local stables available for use by the local stage lines.

This sizable traffic kept the student body well informed on intercolonial news. From the time of the passing of the Stamp Act and through the Revolution there were a series of demonstrations to protest the actions instigated by Great Britain. Following the Stamp Act the students appeared in college in suits made of homespun. Some Philadelphia merchants wrote to the storekeepers in Princeton suggesting that they ignore the nonimport restrictions of the Congress. The students intercepted one of these letters and appeared downtown en masse calling upon the merchants and threatening to burn down their stores if they should attempt to sell imported goods. Furthermore, they engaged a local hangman to burn one of the offensive letters in public while they tolled the university bell.

In January, 1774, inspired by the Boston Tea Party, a group of students seized a shipment of tea which had been sheltered in a warehouse, took it to the public square and burned it. In April, 1776, the British Army under General Howe had landed on the Jersey coast, marched inland, and established headquarters at New Brunswick, which was less than fifty miles from Princeton.

The undergraduates promptly formed a company of fifty men for the defense of the community. This force, though puny, could have the advantage of a delaying action.

Up until the year 1776, the struggle between Great Britain

and the colonies had been sporadic and localized; but the adoption of the Declaration of Independence united the colonies and electrified the world. The Declaration aroused great enthusiasm in the college and town. The document was read aloud in front of the campus. There was a triple volley of muskets and cheers for the prosperity of the new United States.

Howe, in his quarters in New Brunswick, seemingly had not known what to do, but the Declaration roused him to action. He decided to march on Philadelphia, where the Continental Congress was assembled.

President Witherspoon decided that the college must be abandoned for the time being, lest the students all be captured and perhaps even slaughtered. He called an assembly of the students, told them his decision, and advised them to leave the area as promptly as possible. He himself bundled his family into a wagon and set forth for a little community in Pennsylvania which would be accessible to the Continental Congress, in which he was very active.

The war was now right on the threshold of the town and the campus. It may be said that the entire student body was in the colonial armed forces. They had no option to be otherwise. Howe's men pursued a policy of frightfulness. The students were fair game. Nassau Hall was searched for the few men that had remained there. Others were pursued to their boarding houses or other lodgings in the town. Scores were taken prisoner, though their fate in general was not overly serious because Howe wanted to be on the way and not waste time on local skirmishes.

The question of what it felt like to be in the midst of this conflict is illustrated in a letter from Charles Clinton Beatty, class of 1775. to his sister, written from Nassau Hall in May, 1775, shortly before the arrival of Howe's troops.

127

Beatty said, in part:

> How can your patriotic spirit be so dull, when all around is war and bloodshed—certainly you have heard of the skirmishes at Boston, and can you not sympathize with the distressed people there. You need not speak here without it is about Liberty. Every man handles his Musket and hastens his preparations for war. We have a company in College of about 50 officers and all among ourselves, another company they have in town.

The letter continues:

> Our class to show their patriotism intend commencing in Homespun. How I shall get mine I cannot tell, perhaps your goodness can find some scheme. . . .

The same Beatty had intended to enter the ministry, but instead he joined the Army and was accidentally shot by a fellow officer.

Beatty's name appears today in Memorial Hall, which is in the lobby of Nassau Hall. There is a list of those Princeton students who died in the Revolution, a total of ten. The list hardly can be complete, but from biographical sketches of the different classes these are men whose names are matters of record as either ordained ministers or Army officers, sometimes both.

Notable on the list is the name of James Witherspoon, class of 1770. He was the son of President Witherspoon but by no means protected through the influence of his father. On the contrary, he eagerly joined the Patriot armed forces. He was a major, an aide to General Maxwell and again to General Nash. He saw action at Germantown, Pennsylvania, on October 4, 1777, when he was killed.

The town of Princeton and the college buildings were a shambles throughout most of the war period. The British Army took possession of Nassau Hall and was bombarded while located there. A cannon ball went through the portrait of George II, much to the pleasure of the colonials. Considerable damage was done to the college buildings and their equipment. It would be nice to say that when the colonials captured the town they treated the college with respect. Unfortunately his was not the case. They did more damage than the British. They tore up flooring for firewood, knocked down the plaster, and stabled horses on the ground floor.

The tide of victory for the British flowed and ebbed. General Howe had been replaced and had been succeeded by Lord Cornwallis. Cornwallis had been destiny's gift to America because he had the Tory British attitude that the Americans were an inferior lot and that to be beaten by them was unthinkable. Cornwallis led his troops back and forth between New Brunswick and the battles of Princeton and Trenton. Washington was victorious in the major engagements, but in between Cornwallis was supreme at Princeton. While there, he did a thorough job of trying to live off the countryside. He cleaned out all the livestock and provisions of Richard Stockton at Morven and lived for a few months like a prince in that noble establishment, until the American Army returned and drove him out.

But Washington prevailed, and the commencement in 1783 was a triumph for the college. It was attended by George Washington, Lafayette, several diplomats, seven signers of the Declaration, and many members of Congress.

The college had been out of session for most of the war years, but it resumed with renewed strength and with the reputation of having done a great job in the service of the country. Ashbel Green, the valedictorian, in his oration paid tribute to Washington as the man "whose sword taught the tyrants of the earth to fear oppression and opened an asylum for the virtuous and free." It

129

is said that the modest Washington blushed, and when he met Green in the hall the following day he grasped his hand and thanked him.

Green was typical of the young revolutionaries. Starting at the age of sixteen, he had taught school for three years to pay for his college courses. He had finished college in two years. During this scholastic work he had served intermittently in the militia. He ultimately became the eighth president of the college.

Rutgers (Queen's College)

In the year 1776 the young men of New Brunswick, New Jersey, did not need to "go" to war; war came to them. It came in the person of General Howe and his Redcoats, who had established a base at Sandy Hook on the Jersey seacoast from which they began their invasion of New Jersey. They marched inland to New Brunswick, which they occupied until June, 1777.

The British were unwelcome to all elements in the community which were strongly patriotic. The British were especially denounced by the students of Queen's College, which had been started only a few years previously.

To start a college is a hazardous undertaking at any time, but in the unsettled years when Queen's was born its survival was miraculous. New Brunswick, however, was a thriving town, the largest on the road between Elizabeth and Philadelphia. It had many prosperous families, was a trading center, supported three schools and three churches, and had enough business to attract the learned professions. Historian R. P. McCormick reports that by 1770 the city contained "some 150 houses."

The city looked forward to becoming a cultural center, and in 1771 a group of prominent citizens gained the active approval of the governor to start a college; in fact he had granted a charter for it in 1766. Funds were raised, a building was acquired, a tutor was engaged, and classes were started by the fall of that year.

The tutor of the new college was Frederick Frelinghuysen. He was a scion of possibly the most distinguished family in the area, whose roots went back many generations. He had been graduated from the College of New Jersey (Princeton) in the class of 1770. He was soon joined by a classmate, John Taylor, who succeeded him as tutor. In the early days these two men constituted the entire faculty. Each man served at times in combat as an officer with the American Army.

The first commencement of Queen's College was held in October, 1774. There was but one man in the graduating class, but there was a total enrollment of about twenty. The occasion was a triumph over financial adversity, and the college's backers now felt assured of its permanency. That faith was needed, because during the war years the college was obliged to shut down entirely on several occasions and for varying periods.

There was one student organization which gave continuity to the college and leadership to the fighting youth. This was the Athenian Society. It was founded in 1773. It provided a forum for debate and stimulus to literary composition. The group met weekly and discussed such topics of the day as "Liberty" and "The Rising Glory of America." They also read the leading authors, past and present. The minutebook of the society records its sentiments and actions from time to time, for example: "After the landing of General Howe all members of the Athenian Society who were able to bear arms immediately marched to oppose the enemy."

And again, referring to December 1, 1776: "The members of the Athenian Society, still inspired by patriotism, and zealous to promote the interests of America, leaving their peaceable abodes, again

131

assisted their countrymen to repel an enemy endeavoring to establish a system of tyranny and oppression."

Those sentiments are an interesting index both of the British attitude and of the teen-age convictions. The Declaration of Independence was less than six months old, yet the conflict with the home country seemed to be at a stalemate. The Athenian Society boys obviously could not offer a serious threat to Howe. The general in turn seemed to be merely marking time by sitting in New Brunswick. That city had no strategic value except that Howe could use it as a roadblock on the Elizabeth-Philadelphia highway. Howe evidently realized the futility of his position, and in June of the following year (1777) he pulled up his stakes and set out for Philadelphia.

That move was the end of Howe's influence on the affairs of the college except that his occupation had seriously damaged the college properties. The damage presumably was not willful but an inevitable result of army occupation.

The end of the war with Cornwallis' surrender found the college resources nearly exhausted. Virtually all of the alumni had gone to war, the wealth of the community had been drained, and there were only eighteen students in attendance, of whom twelve were freshmen. Taylor assured a friend that he would make a heroic effort to revitalize the college, but this failed. Hence for the years 1784, 1785, and 1786 there were no graduates. Some of the students quietly transferred to other colleges.

The trustees appointed Frelinghuysen to provide classes for any applicants. It is not recorded whether any appeared. Moreover, Frelinghuysen's chief commitments now were to the Continental Congress, the state legislature, various public bodies, and his law practice. He had neglected his private interest for the battlefield and had fought at Princeton, Trenton and Monmouth. At Prince-

132

ton his knowledge of the terrain from his college days had been a conspicuous aid to the Patriot forces.

For nearly forty years it seemed probable that Queen's College would expire and be only a memory of Revolutionary days. Lack of money was the chief worry, augmented by dissension among the college backers. Attempts were made to get contributions from the churches (which yielded only a dribble). Aid was sought from Holland (because of the Dutch population in New Brunswick), and denied. Serious proposals were made for a merger with Princeton (then the College of New Jersey). Finally an adequate plan was underwritten by the local synod of the Dutch Reformed Church.

It was time to change the name of the college, as Queen's was obviously inappropriate. The college president suggested the name of Col. Henry Rutgers. He was a man of great wealth, mostly in Manhattan real estate. He did not make a big contribution to the college, as has been sometimes supposed (he subscribed $5,000 plus $200 to purchase a college bell). But he was a prominent Christian layman whose name would connote virtue and security. The name of Rutgers was adopted unanimously.

William and Mary

William and Mary was the second oldest of the colonial colleges, founded in 1693. Its structure differed from the other colleges. It is not in the area of the New England dissenter group; it was not influenced by the discussion pattern of the Middle Atlantic colleges. It was in style an English university transplanted to America.

The William and Mary curriculum was of the English pattern. Its religion was Church of England. In fact, its original concern with independence had to do with church administration rather than politics. In 1764 the current president, Rev. James Horrocks,

133

advocated the independence of the American Episcopal Church from the Church of England. That was a drastic step which won the approval of many of the laity but was stoutly resisted by many of the clergy.

The proposal was an indication of the thinking of the colonial mind. This rebellious note might have been a warning to the Tory government that the colonial lay mind was not subservient. The clergy of the Church of England owed their appointments to the King. They tended to have Royalist sympathies, and the American appointees rejected the suggestion of Horrocks by a wide margin. If future appointments were to be handled by an American church, the whole security of the situation might be imperiled.

Though Horrocks was defeated on this proposal, the action won him considerable support. He was appointed as rector of the Bruton Parish Church and made a member of the Common Council. Both appointments added to his income. He might well have become a leading figure in the cause of independence. However, he was taken ill and died in 1772, and was succeeded as president of the college by Rev. John Camm. Camm was a conservative and was ousted in 1777 because of his Loyalist views. He did not flee to England as had President Myles Cooper of King's College (Columbia), but retired to his home in York County where he lived as a respected citizen until his death in 1779.

Camm's action was typical of the Virginia attitude. The Virginia citizen desired to be let alone to pursue his own life, and it was not until being repeatedly prodded from abroad that he became ardent for political independence.

Camm, however, was succeeded by Rev. James Madison, a cousin of the future American President. By this time, 1777, when he was only twenty-eight years of age, Madison was an example of the anti-Royalist sentiment of the Colony. It was said that in his sermons he would never speak of heaven as a kingdom, but as: "that great republic where there is no distinction of rank and where all men are free and equal."

Regardless of the fact that the Episcopalian clergy still had ties to the home country, various leaders of the Revolutionary spirit were identified with the college.

W. Melville Jones, dean of the college, affirms that John Marshall, George Wythe, various Randolphs, and George Washington "all were in some way or another associated with the College at the time of the Revolution."

James Monroe, future President of the United States, was perhaps the most famous undergraduate to fight in the colonial cause.

Thomas Jefferson had an influence on the college throughout his life. He attended it in his early years which were pre-Revolutionary, but he had a continuing influence at various stages of his life. He was the principal author of the Declaration of Independence. He advocated many reforms when he was in the Virginia legislature which held its sessions in Williamsburg. He introduced a measure for the abolition of slavery which was rejected. Slaves were a principal form of property in many Virginia estates. He was a chief figure in the abolition of primogeniture. Primogeniture, the inheritance of family property by the firstborn, had been a British principle and had the virtue of keeping property in the same family through generations, but it excluded opportunity for younger sons. Most of the real estate holdings in the New World were in the hands of younger sons who had left England to seek opportunity across the Atlantic. They were receptive to discarding the old ideas.

The college was an early exemplar of friendly relationships with the Indians. Various of the college charters issued by Great Britain

135

described the purpose as: "For the promotion of the Redeemer's name and the British interest." William and Mary, almost from the outset, admitted Indians to their classrooms. These were mostly in the grammar school division, as they were not qualified for higher education. The Indian school provided education for eight to ten persons annually from the beginning of the eighteenth century to 1776. This project was abandoned after American Independence because the source of the endowment supporting it was located in England. On the other hand, the college did offer free scholarships to the sons of the chiefs of the Six Nations. The government promised that they would be well provided for and instructed in all the learning of the white people. The chiefs pondered this offer for a day and then replied:

> We are convinced, therefore, that you mean to do us good by your proposal, and we thank you heartily. But you, who are wise, must know that the different nations have different conceptions of things; and you will therefore not take it amiss if our ideas of this kind of education happen not to be the same with yours. We have had some experience of it. Several of our young people were formerly brought up at the colleges of the northern provinces; they were instructed in all your sciences; but when they came back to us they were bad runners, ignorant of every means of living in the woods, unable to bear either cold or hunger, knew neither how to build a cabin, take a deer, nor kill an enemy, spoke our language imperfectly; were therefore neither fit for hunters, warriors, nor counselors—they were therefore actually good for nothing. We are, however, not the less obliged by your kind offer, though we decline accepting it; and to show our grateful sense of it, if the gentlemen of Virginia will send us a dozen of their sons we will take great care of their education, instruct them in all we know, and make men of them.

The offer of full scholarships had been an extra courtesy intended to enhance mutual friendship. The college catalogue for 1855, which lists visitors (comparable to a board of overseers), and other data as far back as the charter of 1693, names the students "supposed to have been at college after 1720." It also lists the Indians "at the Indian School in 1754." Seven names are given, but all are English Christian names and surnames. The only name suggestive of Indian origin is William Squirrel.

Total attendance at the college in the early 1700's was about thirty, which increased to sixty and totaled about seventy at the start of the Revolution. The college classes from 1755 through 1777 run to a total of more than twenty. After that there was a decided shrinkage, obviously due to the demands of the war.

The catalogue also lists the names of those who "left College during the Revolution to join the American Army." They total twenty-seven and include, in addition to James Monroe (mentioned elsewhere), four Randolphs, two Pages, and two Carters. The list from the catalogue is reproduced in this chapter.

The College of William and Mary, through much of its history, has been a cradle for new ideas. It was a pioneer for the elective system and the honor system. The society of Phi Beta Kappa, which became an honorary scholastic society, was founded at William and Mary in 1776. It sent members to establish chapters at Harvard and Yale, and the society soon became nationwide.

William and Mary, through the succeeding generations, went on to great accomplishments. It established colleges in other parts of the state. It founded a law school and a literary quarterly, and made other advances. However, the major contribution to the pre-Revolutionary movement is the fact that it never adhered to the Royalist position and that it furnished numerous leaders to the Patriot cause.

THE YOUNG REVOLUTIONARIES

The following Students, as appears from the "Virginia Historical Register," left College during the Revolution to join the American Army:

Robert Bolling
Nathaniel Burwell
Otway Byrd
Charles Carter
George Carter
Dandridge Claiborne
Charles Cocke
William Cocke
Langhorne Dade
Edward Digges
Joseph Eggleston
Thomas Evans
Carter B. Harrison
James Lyons

John F. Mercer
James Monroe
William Nelson
Robert Nicholson
Carter Page
Robert Page
David Meade Randolph
Edmund Randolph
Peyton Randolph
Richard Randolph
John Robert
Robert Saunders
Granville Smith

Yale

Yale had as glorious a record as any of the pre-Revolutionary colleges. Without being forced to rebellion as was the Boston area, and with no reluctant leaning toward Royalist authority, Yale and its men embraced the colonial cause from the outset, and heartily. Nathan Hale, of course, was their most notable alumnus. At the name of Nathan Hale, every Yale man could swell with pride.

A young patriot who ultimately became famous along other lines was Noah Webster, author of the dictionary and the famous "Blue-Back Spellers." At the age of twenty, he enlisted with several of his classmates at Yale and started out with a small company prepared to fight Burgoyne, who was expected to march his army to Albany. As historians know, Burgoyne was forced to surrender to the Continentals long before he reached Albany. Never-

138

theless, Noah endured all the discomforts of soldiers on the march, without having an opportunity for glory. His diary complains about poor food, damp ground at night, and lack of sleep, and is a realistic account of the fact that warfare is no fun. Still he persevered, as did dozens of his classmates. In fact, Yale undergraduates were so largely committed to the cause that the campus was almost deserted, and the college did not return to normality until ultimately peace had been declared.

The college for six years abandoned any attempt to occupy the New Haven campus. Classes were held wherever there might be a safe location. Yale became an idea, a talisman. The college would stand; there was no thought of abandoning it. The colonies would win; that was the sure thought. At the end Yale would rise in its pristine glory as one of the great educational institutions of the united colonies.

Bibliography

Alexander, Samuel Davies, *Princeton College During the XVIII Century*. New York, Anson D. F. Randolph & Co., 1872.

Allan, Herbert S., *John Hancock, Patriot in Purple*. New York, Macmillan, 1948.

Atherton, Gertrude F., *The Conqueror, Being the True and Romantic Story of Alexander Hamilton*. New York, Macmillan, 1902.

Boatner, Mark Mayo, III, *Encyclopedia of the American Revolution*. New York, David McKay, 1966.

Brant, Irving, *James Madison, The Virginia Revolutionist*. New York, Bobbs-Merrill, 1941.

Bronson, Walter C., *The History of Brown University, 1764–1914*, Providence, Brown University, 1914.

Brubacher, John S., *Higher Education in Transition*. New York, Harper & Bros., 1958.

Buell, Augustus C., *History of Andrew Jackson*. New York, Scribner's, 1904.

Catalogue of William and Mary College, in the State of Virginia, 1855. Williamsburg, J. Hervey Ewing, Printer.

Collins, V. L., *President Witherspoon*. Princeton, Princeton University Press, 1925.

Dictionary of American Biography, Dumas Malone, ed. New York, Scribner's, 1936.

The Dictionary of National Biography. Sir Leslie Stephen and Sir Sidney Lee, ed. Oxford, Oxford University Press, reprinted 1959–1960.

Foote, Rev. William Henry, *Sketches of North Carolina*. New York, Robert Carter, 1846.

General Catalogue of Princeton University, 1746–1906. Princeton, Princeton University Press, 1908.

Gerson, Noel B., *Light-Horse Harry*. Garden City, Doubleday, 1966. Biography of Henry Lee.

Yankee Doodle Dandy. Garden City, Doubleday, 1965. Biographical novel of John Hancock.

James, Marquis, *Andrew Jackson, the Border Captain*. Indianapolis, Bobbs-Merrill, 1933.

Keppel, Frederick Paul, *Columbia*. New York, Oxford University Press, 1914.

Lippincott, Horace Mather, *The University of Pennsylvania*. Philadelphia, Lippincott, 1919.

The Lives of Eighteen from Princeton. Willard Thorp, ed. Princeton, Princeton University Press, 1946.

McCormick, Richard P., *Rutgers: A Bicentennial History*. New Brunswick, Rutgers University Press, 1966.

Memorial Quadrangle, A Book About Yale. Robert Dudley French, compiler. New Haven, Yale University Press, 1929.

Mitchell, Broadus, *Alexander Hamilton, Youth to Maturity*. New York, Macmillan, 1962.

Moore, N. F., *An Historical Sketch of Columbia College*. New York, Columbia College, 1846.

Morison, Samuel Eliot, *Three Centuries of Harvard*. Cambridge, Harvard University Press, 1936.

142

BIBLIOGRAPHY

Parton, James, *Life of Andrew Jackson*. New York, Mason Bros., 1860.

Pier, Arthur Standwood, *The Story of Harvard*. Boston, Little, Brown, 1913.

Quint, Wilder D., *The Story of Dartmouth*. Boston, Little, Brown, 1914.

Riethmuller, Christopher James, *The Life and Times of Alexander Hamilton*. London, Bell, 1864.

Rives, William C., *History of the Life and Times of James Madison*. Boston, Little Brown, 1859.

Sargent, Winthrop, *The Life and Career of Major John André*. New York, William Abbatt, 1902.

Schmidt, George P., *Princeton and Rutgers*. Princeton, Van Nostrand, 1964.

Stanley, Dean, *Memorials of Westminster Abbey*. London, Westminster Abbey, undated.

Stone, Irving, *Those We Love*. New York, Doubleday, 1965.

Twentieth Century Biographical Dictionary of Notable Americans. Boston, Biographical Society, 1904.

Two Centuries of Christian Activity at Yale. James B. Reynolds, Samuel H. Fisher, and Henry B. Wright, ed. New York, Putnam, 1901.

Tyler, Lyon G., *The College of William and Mary in Virginia: Its History and Work, 1693–1907*. Richmond, Whittet & Shepperson, Printers, 1907.

Walsh, James J., *Educating the Founding Fathers of the Republic*. New York, Fordham University Press, 1935.

Wertenbaker, Thomas Jefferson, *Princeton, 1746–1896*. Princeton, Princeton University Press, 1946.

Wood, George B., M.D., *Early History of the University of Pennsylvania*. Philadelphia, Lippincott, 1896.